READING THE GOOD NEWS IN GALILEE

READING
THE GOOD NEWS
IN GALILEE

by

GEORGE HAKIM
Archbishop of Galilee

HELICON
Baltimore – Dublin

Helicon Press, Inc.
1120 N. Calvert Street
Baltimore, Maryland, 21202

Helicon Limited
53 Capel Street
Dublin 1, Ireland

Nihil Obstat: CARROLL E. SATTERFIELD
Censor Liborum

Imprimatur: ✠LAWRENCE CARDINAL SHEHAN
Archbishop of Baltimore
February 24, 1965

The *Nihil Obstat* and *Imprimatur* are official declarations that a book or pamphlet is free of doctrinal or moral error. No implication is contained therein that those who have granted the *Nihil Obstat* and *Imprimatur* agree with the opinions expressed.

Originally published in French under the title *Pages d'Évangile lues en Galilée* by Éditions E. Vercrusse-Vanhove, Saint-André-Bruges.

Translated by James A. Corbett

PRINTED IN THE REPUBLIC OF IRELAND BY
HELY THOM LIMITED, DUBLIN

FOREWORD

During his visit to the United States in the summer of 1964, His Grace George Hakim, Archbishop of Galilee (Israel), encouraged the Melkites, Maronites, Armenians and Copts "to affirm proudly their adhesion to their respective Oriental Rites, the very existence of which in the Church are a manifestation of her catholicity, and bring to Western Christianity an echo of the theological thinking and mystical life of the Patristic Age, close to the times of our Lord's coming among us."

His Grace George Hakim has the privilege both of being bishop of the First Diocese, one might say, of the Church— that founded in the Holy Land by Peter and James—and of belonging to the branch of the Eastern Rite Church in union with Rome. His spirituality is thus firmly rooted in the land of our Lord and on the shores of the Bosporus. It has an affinity with Byzantium and with the Supreme See of Rome. No wonder, then, that he impresses his listeners by the profoundness of his words of edification and above all by his interest in all men and his fatherly appearance. He has the genius of awakening each Christian to the life of grace, that of the "interior man" who seeks to establish in his heart "the kingdom of God".

Archbishop Hakim was born May 18, 1908 in Egypt. He studied at the Jesuit College in Cairo, then at St. Anne's Seminary at Jerusalem conducted by the White Fathers of the African Mission. After his ordination on July 20, 1930 he was Superior of the Patriarchal School in Cairo for nine years. Because of his remarkable personality and competence he was consecrated Archbishop of Acre, Nazareth and Galilee on June 13, 1943. He was only thirty-five years of age. Since then he has built many churches, a convent, an orphanage, a seminary and developed a vast apostolic activity extending far beyond his diocese. He is the founder of two Arabic magazines and author of the fascinating and inspiring book entitled, in its French edition, "Gospel Pages Read in Galilee". It is here presented to the American public under the title of *Reading the Good News in Galilee*.

There is much to learn from these pages. They are written in a simple style with the aim of bringing us closer to the holy humanity of Jesus of Nazareth by introducing us to the country of his origin and inciting in us the feeling and thought of its people. One has to have lived many years in that land and cherished its customs wholeheartedly to succeed in doing this so perfectly.

The Rt. Rev. Elias Denissoff, Archimandrite
An Archpriest of the Diocese of Galilee

PREFACE

In reading the Gospels everyone quite naturally understands them in the light of his own outlook and background. Almost unconsciously one is led to apply the experiences of his own milieu to the various family scenes or manifestations of every day life they contain. This raises certain difficulties however.

Happily, numerous recent publications have given us many new insights. Today more people realize that we must read the gospels, like all historical works, in a human context which the increasing number of pilgrimages and travellers have made easier for us to grasp.

Villages are more conservative than towns, and they have maintained many local customs and ways which tourists, or travellers in a hurry, have difficulty in discovering. These traditions are tending, however, to disappear as "modern civilization" permeates the countryside. Yet these old ways do clarify many obscure points of holy scripture. The customs we are about to describe are those of contemporary Arab villages, whether Christian or Moslem. As Oriental Jewish customs do not differ very much from Arab customs, I believe we can discover certain characteristics of life as it was lived in the time of our Lord by observing contemporary village life. It would be wrong to ask modern Jews, who are for the most part very Europeanized, to explain the way of life of the first century.

Before publishing this book its chapters were given as talks to a restricted circle of friends. They have no other purpose than to reveal the simple flavor of the gospels, to bring Jesus closer to us, as he lived in his environment, without the numerous complications which have been added and which do not make him more lovable.

I have avoided all the theological and exegetical difficulties which are not the object of this book. This is not a work of erudition such as those books written in recent years by scholars, who have had so many wonderful things to say about sacred scripture.

It would be advisable for a reader to have the gospel text before him as he follows the comments made in this book.

I would like to thank here all those who have co-operated in going over the text, and those who have helped in getting it ready.

To those who read this book, my friends or those unknown to me, I would like to say this: I hope that when you finish reading you will feel that you understand the gospel a little better and thus love it more. If you feel that you are nearer to Jesus than you had been; if you feel "your heart leap" in imitation of the disciples at Emmaus, and you decide to "stop with him" and become in your own time and place and circumstances a devout apostle of the Nazarene—then I will have the joy and the consolation of telling myself that, in my very simplicity, I have helped in bringing you to share in the life and in the attractive appeal of this little bit of ground which, in the immensity of his creation, the Christ willed to reserve in order to make it his country, the Holy Land.

✠GEORGE HAKIM
Archbishop of Galilee

Nazareth

CONTENTS

Contents

PART I

THE COUNTRY HE CHOSE

CHAPTER ONE

THE LAY OF THE LAND

Palestine is that tiny corner of the world today occupied by the state of Israel and the Hashemite kingdom of Jordan. The latter, formerly "Trans-Jordan" (east of the Jordan), now includes that part of Arab Palestine west of the Jordan not occupied by the state of Israel.

Galilee—the land of Nazareth, Cana, Mt. Tabor, the Lake of Tiberias, Capharnaum, the Mount of the Beatitudes —is wholly in Israel.

The chief holy places of Judea—apart from Mount Sion, the Cenacle, and Ain-Karim which are in Israel—are in Jordan: Bethlehem, Hebron, old Jerusalem and the Mount of Olives, Jericho, Sichem and Jacob's well.

On a relief map, Palestine consists of a number of plains along the west coast, several mountain ranges in the center, and, to the east, the Jordan in its valley, called in Arabic the *Ghor* ("deep hollow"). In this valley more extensive hollows form the Lake of Tiberias in the north and the Dead Sea in the south.

These three parts of Palestine call for somewhat more detailed treatment.

THE PLAINS

From north to south, except for the small hill of Carmel in

the neighborhood of Haifa, there stretches a series of moderate-sized plains. The best known of these are the "Plain of Sharon" in the north and the "Plain of Sephela or of the Philistines" in the south. These fertile plains, formerly inhabited by non-Jews, do not seem to have been visited by our Lord—except the easternmost part of the Plain of Sephela, between the coastal plain and the hill country, where Emmaus may have been located.

On the other hand, the rich plain of Esdrelon, between the mountains of Galilee and those of Samaria, seems to have lain along the route usually taken by the Holy Family on its way from Nazareth to Jerusalem, Bethlehem or Ain-Karim. Moreover, it is full of reminders of all the wars of antiquity, since it is the only suitable battlefield between the Taurus mountains in the north and the *Negeb* (Hebr., "dry") desert in the south.

MOUNTAINS

Three mountain ranges mark the middle of the map of Palestine:

(*a*) the mountains of Galilee, in the north; these are the lowest mountains in Palestine, except at Safad, on the northern frontier, where they rise to almost four thousand feet. The two Galilean hills most important historically are Carmel (from about a thousand to sixteen hundred feet in altitude), famous as the scene of the Prophet Elias' holocaust (3 Kings 18) and Tabor (1,929 feet), where our Lord was transfigured before the three dazzled disciples.

(*b*) the mountains of Samaria, whose two most celebrated peaks are about three thousand feet high (Ebal, 3,084 feet;

The Mount of Olives

Jacob's Well near Nablus

The Garden of Gethsemane

The Virgin's Fountain in Nazareth

Garizim, 2,890 feet). Nearby is "Jacob's well" or "the well of the Samaritan woman."

(*c*) the mountains of Judea, in the midst of which are perched Jerusalem, Bethlehem and Hebron, rise from three to four thousand feet in altitude. The Mount of Olives near Jerusalem is 2,723 feet in altitude at its highest point.

The gospels indicate Jesus' movements between these various mountains, in remarkably precise terms.

Speaking of our Lord's movements in Galilee, the gospel remarks that he "went about in Galilee" (John 7:1). On the other hand, it speaks of him going "*up* to Jerusalem" and "*down* to Capharnaum" (Mark 10:32; Luke 4:31; John 2:12–13; 7:10 etc.). One has the vivid impression that the writers had also at times gone "up" or "down" in long caravans, travelling on foot and sometimes in weather by no means pleasant!

Only once does the gospel speak of Jesus passing through Samaria, inhabited as it was by a people half-Jew and half-pagan who were despised by the Pharisees and other pious Jews. The gospel uses a very precise expression, "He had to pass through Samaria" (John 4: 4), thereby indicating the exceptional character of this visit to a country ordinarily avoided by Jews, but where Christ would be very cordially welcomed (John 4:40–42). Usually he "was passing between Samaria and Galilee" (Luke 17:11), that is, between the two provinces, to reach the Jordan, the "Ghor," down which he would travel as far as Jericho and from there up to Jerusalem.

We might remark in passing that the Samaritans in the gospel are depicted in a very favorable light. Apart from the contemptuous insult "You are a Samaritan" (John 8:48)

2

and the Samaritan village mentioned in Luke 9:51–56, nothing discreditable is recorded of them. They are fine people.

It is the *good* Samaritan (Luke 10:25 ff.) whom our Lord uses as an example to teach us the lesson of brotherly love: to dismount on the deserted mountain road halfway between Jerusalem and Jericho certainly called for unheard-of charity! After such an example, our Lord could say indeed: "love your enemies" (Matthew 5:44). Again, it was to a *Samaritan* woman that our Lord made revelations of the highest importance: "I am the Messias," he told her (John 4:26). This is the only time such a revelation is made so clearly. It is also a Samaritan who appears in the best light among the ten lepers cured by our Lord, who in turn even goes out of his way to emphasize the fact for the benefit of his Jewish audience: "Were not the ten made clean? . . . Where are the other nine? Has no one been found to return to give glory to God except this foreigner!" (Luke 17:11–19).

RIVERS

The most important river of Palestine is the Jordan, in which John baptized and in which our Lord received the baptism with which he began his public life. This little river, aside from its biblical and evangelical importance, is lower lying than any other in the world. In its short course it traverses practically unparalleled extremes of altitude. At its source, near Baniyas (Caesarea Philippi) it is at an altitude of about twenty-five hundred feet, at Lake Hula it is six feet below sea-level, but where it empties into the Dead Sea, it is 1,286 feet below sea-level.

One of the Jordan's most important tributaries, the Yarmuck, in Transjordan, is probably in the neighborhood of the place where John was baptizing.[1] We must also mention two small rivers: the Cedron and the Kishon.

The Cedron, a small stream that flows between Jerusalem and the Mount of Olives, was crossed by the group of apostles as they went from the supper room to Gethsemane on the evening of Holy Thursday.

The Kishon, the "Mokattah" to the Arabs (i.e., "slashed," because of the numerous zigzags that it traces in its short course), flows at the foot of Carmel, near Haifa. The Bible tells us that the blood of five hundred priests of Baal, slaughtered by the prophet Elias, mingled with the waters of this stream and turned it completely red.

---

[1] In recent years the Jordan and the Yarmuk have acquired world-wide notoriety on account of the interest shown in them by the Great Powers. This interest is manifested in concrete form in the proposed "Johnston plan" for dredging and straitening the streams and dividing their waters between the adjoining countries.

t years the Jordan and the Yarmuk have acquired
 notoriety on account of the interest shown in them by
 eat Powers. This interest is manifested in concrete form in the
 oposed "Johnston plan" for dredging and straitening the streams
and dividing their waters between the adjoining countries.

CHAPTER TWO

CLIMATE

The whole life of our Lord was affected by the special climate of Palestine. Thus, in order to understand a multitude of little details referred to in the gospel, it is necessary to have some accurate ideas on this subject.

SEASONS

In Palestine there are really only two seasons: winter, the rainy season (from November to April), and summer, when rain is almost unknown. The warmest weather ("Khamsin")[2] comes with the east wind, and follows without fail immediately upon winter (April and May). Towards mid-October, some days of *Khamsin* and of very oppressive heat announce the end of summer.

The gospel knows only these two seasons. Our Lord speaks of the fig tree: "When its branch is now tender, and the leaves break forth"—a phenomenon that takes place ordinarily in March—"you know that summer is near" (Matthew 24:32).

---

2. The Arabic word *Khamsin*, which means fifty, signifies a period of fifty days, during which the east wind brings with it heat and dust. This period occurs in April and May but has intervals of three or four days at a time when the air is fresh and cool.

The public life of our Lord unfolds for the most part in Galilee during the summer, and most often in Juda during the winter. Here, in the porches of the temple, he had a shelter where the people could listen to him: "Now there took place at Jerusalem the feast of the Dedication; and it was winter [mid-December]. And Jesus was walking in the temple, in Solomon's porch" (John 10:22).

The Jewish holydays have been worked out in terms of the climate: Passover falls at the end of winter (the end of March or the beginning of April); the feast of Tabernacles is located at the beginning of winter, and it is a good omen if it coincides with the first rains. In between the two is Pentecost: the time of harvest and of the firstfruits.

If we use a synopsis such as that by Lagrange and Lavergne, and perhaps a historical atlas of the New Testament, it is easy to follow our Lord when we read the gospels. He made several journeys in Juda (winter and Passover), and spent the summers in Galilee.

He drove the money-changers out of the temple, and had the conversation with Nicodemus, in March during the first year of his public life. The events which accompanied the feast of Tabernacles (end of October) and those from the feast of Dedication until the Passover, when he was crucified, took place during the winter of the third year of his public life, with an interval in Perea and the Jordan valley.

Apart from these periods, our Lord was in Galilee where the fields were gayer, nature in a more smiling mood, and the people more receptive, even though it was likely to be much hotter than in Judea.

RAIN AND HEAT

Rain has always been and still is a source of blessing for those parts of Palestine where it falls. Where no rain falls there is the desert, the dry land. When there is insufficient rainfall, crops are poor; scarcity and famine result.

Only modern techniques have made the digging of artesian wells feasible or made it possible to think of turning the waters of the Jordan to profitable use. Perhaps the time will come when rainfall will be less important. But at least up to now, it is essential for the survival of life and civilizations. The Eastern Church provides for special prayers to be said when the rains are late in coming or inadequate when they do come.

It is in the light of all this that we are to understand our Lord's words when he says of his heavenly Father that he "sends rain on the just and the unjust" (Matthew 5:45). Among the gifts of heaven, rain is the most important for the people of those parts.

Snow, which is occasionally seen nowadays on the mountains of Judea during an exceptionally severe winter, does not seem to have been mentioned in the gospels. But there are allusions to the rigors of winter: witness the soldiers warming themselves around the fire and Peter feeling the need to join them (Mark 14:67; John 18:25). And yet winter was supposed to be over at the time of the Passover.

Dew, which is of considerable importance, especially for fruit trees, makes up in some measure for the lack of rain. The Bible likens dew in abundance to an act of charity (cf. Psalms 132:3).

During the summer, our Lord must have known in his
travels the heat and humidity which we experience today—
sometimes more than 100° in the shade. The days of the
Khamsin, during which the east wind, laden with burning
sand, blows across the country are extremely disagreeable.
Fortunately these come only during a few weeks at the
beginning of summer and alternate with intervals of three
to seven days of cooler weather. During the summer the
humidity along the coast and the heat in the *Ghor* are, of
course, more oppressive than what is to be found in the
mountains. But here and there cooler nights relieve the
hardships of summer and make the season more tolerable.

During the hot season, the only thirst-quenching and
pleasant drink is water—provided it is cold. Thus, when
our Lord speaks of the reward promised to "whoever gives
to one of these little ones but a cup of cold water to drink,"
he is careful to specify that it be cold (Matthew 10:42). And
offering a drink of cold water calls for some effort: you have
to go to a fountain or draw the water fresh from the cistern,
which presupposes, in either case, a certain amount of
trouble and a measure of delicacy in the performance of an
act of charity. Because of this willingness to put oneself out
"he shall not lose his reward."

It must surely have been on a *Khamsin* day that our
Lord, "wearied as he was from the journey, was sitting at
the well" (John 4:6). The evangelist is exact: "It was about
the sixth hour," that is, noon. And how natural it is that
his first words to the Samaritan woman who had come "to
draw water" should be "give me to drink."

The whole ensuing conversation beautifully follows out
this theme of thirst. It was, to be sure, a real and burning

thirst—the Samaritan woman persisted in looking at it in a material way, whereas all the while Jesus was thinking of a thirst for justice and eternal life. At any other time than a *Khamsin* day, such a conversation would not be so pointed.

Today, as in the first century, the words of the gospel have the ring of truth: "When you see a cloud rising in the west, you say at once: 'A shower is coming'; and so it comes to pass. And when you see the south wind blow, you say: 'There will be a scorching heat'; and so it comes to pass" (Luke 12:54–55).

Finally, in this connection, we shall say a word about the clearness of the sky in the East. A magnificent blue during the day, at night (often even during winter) it shines with myriads of stars set in its limpid clarity. This extraordinary clearness of the sky has been, both in ancient and modern times, an inducement to watchers of the sky, who have never been lacking in the Orient. It also enables us to understand more readily the text of Matthew (2:7, 9) about the star of the Magi.

WATER

At the present time, extensive projects of irrigation and well-digging are being planned or have already been completed.

In former times—and even today in a great many villages—the people of Palestine had no other source of drinking water than rainfall, which was gathered in cisterns or wells frequently hollowed out of the rock itself. It is easy, therefore, to understand the importance people attached to these wells.

This or that great personage achieved immortality by

building pyramids, formulating a famous code of laws, constructing one or other of the seven wonders of the world; in Palestine, Jacob's name lives on and is held in blessing down through the centuries because he dug a well (John 4:6). No pilgrimage to Palestine is complete without a visit to "Jacob's well," a mile or so from Nablus. Not far from Ebal and Garazim, it could gather all the water that drained from them. And apparently it never fills up, for the water level is always the same when the custodian lowers into it a little bucket at the end of a rope almost a hundred feet long. This "well of Jacob" is the silent witness of the conversation between Jesus and the Samaritan woman (John 4).

The importance of cisterns will be more clearly realized, if we consider this little fact: not long ago when a new church in memory of the Prophet Elias was to be built at Isfia on Mount Carmel, the first thing done was to dig a cistern and then wait for it to fill with a winter's rains before the actual work of construction could go on the next summer. Otherwise it would have been necessary to bring water from Haifa, nearly ten miles away.

It was and still is the task of young girls to bring water from the springs or wells.

The holy Virgin had to perform the tasks that one can see being done today, very often at daybreak, by all the young girls and married women, at Nazareth, at Cana, and at many other places.

And it is easy to understand how lightened would be the burden of a woman who no longer had to go to a well to draw water: "Sir, give me this water that I may not thirst, or come here to draw," the woman said to him (John 4:15).

According to custom it is the women who are the porters of water. They carry the precious liquid in pitchers, balanced on their heads. In certain sections, if a man carries water he will not carry it in a pitcher, but in a goatskin fastened to his back.

And so we realize that our Lord can give the apostles an unmistakable sign: "a man carrying a pitcher of water" (Mark 14:13). This exception can only make the task of the two apostles easier, for they could not be mistaken. With this prophecy they would at once be able to single out this unique water-carrier from all the many other water-carriers. "Go into the city, and there you will meet a man carrying a pitcher of water; follow him."

You would not make a mistake; there could be only one!

CHAPTER THREE

CROPS

CEREALS

Wheat, barley, sesame, lentils. . . . In the little villages today, everyone cultivates a bit of land. And some of the villagers also follow a trade: carpenters, blacksmiths, stone-masons.

Since these tradesmen do not find enough customers in their own village or the neighboring villages to provide them with a year-round livelihood, they work their little plots of ground. In the months when they are not busy sowing or harvesting, they ply their trade. Moreover, it is from his trade that the name by which a man is ordinarily known comes. Thus, we speak of "the carpenter," "the carpenter's son," and so on.

It must have been this way in the hamlet of Nazareth in our Lord's day. Joseph the carpenter must have had his little plot of ground that he worked with his "son" to make a living, whenever his carpenter's trade left him any free time. It is reasonable then to suppose that Jesus, "Joseph the carpenter's son," also worked on the land, and that when he spoke of the sower, of the harvest, the growing wheat, and the like, he would speak from personal experience, as one who knew what he was talking about. Thus, in Mark 4:3–9, 26–30, our Lord describes the growth of the ears of wheat as a very good observer: "The seed

should sprout . . . the earth bears the crop, first the blade,
then the ear, then the full grain in the ear." The gospel
does not seem to refer to any other grains but wheat and
barley.

It should be noted that the soil is less fertile now than in
our Lord's time, and produces a smaller yield: a return of
twenty for one is very unusual. A normal season will bring
a return of from seven to ten for one; and it can be reasonably surmised that even in our Lord's day, the "hundredfold" must have been a wonderful exception.[3]

The peasants practically never use fertilizers; instead they
let the ground lie fallow every other year. They jealously
hoard the seed that is to be used the following year and, if
necessary, they will sell their clothes rather than use up
their seed.

In many places the methods of cultivation are still very
primitive; the ploughshare digs a furrow hardly more than
eight or twelve inches deep. The farmer is not upset by the
brambles or stones that dot his fields; rather than take the
trouble to remove them, he just goes round them with his
plough.

In the life of the people nowadays, their free time comes
especially between the planting season after the first rains
(November and December) and the harvest (June): Lent
and Easter come during this period. Also after the crops are
in (Pentecost) and during a part of the summer (the feast of
Tabernacles) they have some free time. Public meetings are
unthinkable during planting or harvest time. The most that

---

3. Such an exception is reported in the Bible, twenty centuries
previously: "And Isaac sowed in that land, and he found that same
year a hundredfold" (Gen 26:12—Douay).

can be expected is that the little children and a few oldsters will come to Mass in the villages at these times.

It must have been the same way in our Lord's time: in the gospel, his apostolic preaching and his travels took place, almost exclusively, about Passover time or the feast of Pentecost or Tabernacles.

FRUIT TREES

The principal fruits raised in Palestine are figs, olives, palms, carobs, vines and oranges. They are all mentioned in the gospel except the orange.

The fig tree, whose leaves come out in March, is the harbinger of summer: "From the fig tree learn this parable. When its branch is now tender, and the leaves break forth, you know that summer is near" (Mark 13:28).

The fig tree's barrenness was cursed because it was the symbol of the Pharisees' unbelief (Matthew 21:19) and also because it uselessly took up space in the father's field: "And he said to the vine-dresser, 'Behold, for three years now I have come seeking fruit on this fig tree, and I find none. Cut it down, therefore; why does it still encumber the ground?'" (Luke 13:7).

Is is easy to understand this reaction of a property owner who has only a few good bits of soil in his rocky field and sees a useless tree taking up valuable room there! A good many people are in the same situation even today.

The olive, with which the "Mount of Olives" was covered, whose branches were probably used during the Messiah's triumphal entry into Jerusalem, is still very extensively cultivated today. Olive oil and olives themselves provide an important part of the diet of the Arabs. The olive thrives in certain parts of Galilee and Judea, but there is hardly an Arab village without at least a few trees. Very hardy, the olive can survive the bad seasons which bring no rain, and usually bears fruit only every other year.

The palm, which is becoming more and more rare in populated areas, is still plentiful in some desert regions, especially in the south. Its branches were also used at the triumphal entry of our Lord into Jerusalem. Only John mentions this explicitly: "The great crowd . . . took the branches of palms and went forth to meet him, and they cried out, 'Hosanna! Blessed is he who comes in the name of the Lord, the king of Israel!' " (John 12:13).

The carob tree, the fruit of which the prodigal son wanted to eat, is also a tree that is resistant to all sorts of weather, and which does not require much care.

Just as today in the state of Israel, as a result of the pressure of Orthodox Jews, the raising of swine is forbidden in Jewish areas and restricted to non-Jewish villages, we can likewise suppose that the prodigal son had to go "to a far country," perhaps to one of the pagan towns of the Decapolis: "The younger son . . . took his journey into a far country; and there he squandered his fortune in loose living . . . And he longed to fill himself with the [carob] pods that the swine were eating, but no one offered to give them to him" (Luke 15:11–16).

The sycamore is becoming more and more rare in Palestine. Very common in Egypt, it resembles the fig tree, but its leaves are broader and more thick-set. A small man like Zaccheus could easily have hidden in a sycamore tree and not have been noticed. "He was small of stature. So

The Tomb of the Virgin and the Grotto of Gethsemane

The Mosque of Omar (The Dome of the Rock)

Children of Galilee

PHOTO: LABORATORIO FOTO ZINCOGRAPHICO

he ran on ahead and climbed up into a sycamore tree, for he was going to pass that way" (Luke 19:1–10).

The vine, which together with the olive is still today one of the most important sources of revenue, unquestionably enjoys an unparalleled prominence in the gospel not only because it is the source of the wine so frequently mentioned, but also because it furnishes the basis for the wonderful allegory developed in Chapter 15 of John.

Nothing is more moving, even today, than a walk by night from the Cenacle to Gethsemane, where pilgrims and the devout of Jerusalem love to spend long hours the night of Holy Thursday.

We relive in a touching manner those tragic moments in which our Lord, after the institution of the Holy Eucharist and the priesthood, leaves the Cenacle, followed by his eleven anxious disciples. The moon was full. Going down the slope of Mt. Sion toward the Cedron, he calls attention to the vines. The thick stocks are almost bare; the tiny leaves are only beginning to bud at the beginning of April. Bundles of recently pruned dead branches lie nearby and will provide fuel for baking bread and preparing meals on the present-day *taboun*. [4]

In opposition to many better qualified exegetes, I think that there is a perfectly consistent sequence of ideas between the fourteenth and fifteenth chapters of St. John: Getting up from the table after the Last Supper, Jesus says to his disciples: "Arise; let us go from here." They all go out and down toward the Cedron along the footpath that follows

---

4. Small structures of beaten earth which take the place of bake-houses in the villages.

the drop of the wall. The hillside is planted with vines, which Jesus can see quite clearly in the moonlight. Apparently he points to them as he continues speaking, walking slowly: "I am the true vine, and my Father is the vine-dresser."

Seeing the dry branches that had been cut off and tied up in bundles for the fire, he adds quite naturally, "As the branch cannot bear fruit of itself unless it remain on the vine, so neither can you unless you abide in me."

With a first-hand knowledge of the terrain involved we can try to understand better the parable in Mark 12:1–11:

"A man planted a vineyard." It is normal procedure to plant vines on the sides of a hill, in the midst of the ever-present rocks—where the planting of grain is out of the question—in order to get some return from the bit of ground he has. In recent years, when fruit has been bringing better prices than grains, the price of which has risen only slightly, even fine level tracts have been planted in vines.

The first thing to do after planting a vineyard is to protect it against animals (goats, jackals) by putting "a hedge about it," a hedge of heaps of stones, thistles, thorn-bushes, and so on. Later, you "dig a wine vat" in the rock itself, in the middle of the property, with a channel to carry off the grapejuice. When the grapes are ripening in summer, the owner puts up a "tower," a platform resting on wooden supports six or seven feet high. On this he strews branches and leaves to provide a bed where he spends the night. From this observation post he can protect his vineyard against marauders and wild animals and at the same time enjoy the coolness of the eastern night.

If the owner is rich and can afford to travel or wants a

change—Orientals are born nomads[5]—he "leases out" his property to vine-dressers and at the time of the vintage he sends "a servant . . . to receive . . . some of the fruit of the vineyard." Nowadays this share is about one-third of the yield, the other two-thirds going to those who have taken care of the vineyard, unless the owner has helped to take care of the expenses of cultivation, in which case he gets half of the fruits.

WILD PLANTS

In Palestine there are a great number of bushes, thorns and thistles that cover the many mountains and at times even crowd into the midst of the fields.

Our Lord had seen them very often, and no doubt had tried to uproot some of them in his bit of ground on the outskirts of Nazareth. He knew them quite well.

These fierce thickets that drained the earth without giving fruit were like false prophets: "Beware of false prophets . . . By their fruits you will know them. Do men gather grapes from thorns, or figs from thistles? . . . Every tree that does not bear good fruit is cut down and thrown into the fire" (Matthew 7:15–20).

The crown of thorns (Matthew 17:29) must have been plaited from the spiny bushes so abundant in the neighborhood of Jerusalem, which the soldiers had gathered for their fire.

FLOWERS

The flowers which thrust their way up naturally today at

---

5. "Even the lame man from Aleppo has been as far as China," says an Arab proverb.

winter's end make Palestine, and above all Galilee, look
like a carpet dyed with colorful greenery. They must have
been seen often by our Lord, and were well known to him:
anemones, tulips, cyclamen, wild lilies always white. "See
how the lilies of the field grow," says our Lord, ". . . I say
to you that not even Solomon in all his glory was arrayed
like one of these"(Matthew 6:28–29).

In their extreme poverty, men are anxious about what
they shall eat and how they shall clothe themselves (Matthew
6:25). Women will wonder, especially toward the end of
summer, if they will have a sufficient supply of water,
particularly if the rains have not been abundant the preceding winter. Starting out from the things before their eyes
and under foot, the Master invites them to "not be anxious
about tomorrow" (Matthew 6:34).

CHAPTER FOUR

HOUSES

Dwelling-places in our own day vary from luxurious villas to tiny huts.

Attractive buildings of stone, the skyscrapers of certain great cities of the East, and the display of recent villas, equal in every way the best buildings of the West.

But in the villages houses of more than one storey are not often to be seen. These dwelling-places are usually cubes, with the entrance as the only opening, and generally low.

The poorest villagers live in caves hollowed out of the rock. In front of these the occupants build a barrier out of stones and old crates and tin cans, and in this an entrance way is placed. If ever they have to move, they never fail to carry off with them their "front door," undoubtedly one of the most important items of their personal property.

Sanitary installations, running water and all the convenience it allows, are scarcely known in the villages.

In the time of our Lord, it must have been the same: luxury and poverty dwelling side by side!

The remains of monumental buildings that our Lord must have seen have been discovered today. These witness to a wealth of architectural and material construction hardly surpassed by us today. These include, among others, the foundations of the temple, Herod's palace, and the foundations of the Procurator's Pool, which can be admired at Jerusalem.

But alongside these monumental edifices there are the hovels of the poor. Often these are built from some of the stones that they have found here and there, but quite as often they are grottoes carved in the side of the hills.

Our Lord, and the holy family, no doubt lived in just such grottoes. It is this fact that allows us to identify more or less successfully most of the sites which they recall to our devotion.

Although their authenticity is not always certain, through the centuries Christians have built on these grottoes the monuments we venerate today: the Grotto of the Nativity of our Lord at Bethlehem, the Grotto of the Nativity of Mary at Jerusalem, the Grotto of the Nativity of John the Baptist at Ain-Karim, the Grotto of the Annunciation at Nazareth, and so forth.

In the light of these observations certain gospel texts, which at first sight present difficulties, can be seen more clearly. And we see that they reveal, as always, a very great exactness.

DESCRIPTIONS — GOSPEL TEXTS

Let us simply read what the various texts say with regard to the birth of Christ:

Luke 2:7: "She brought her firstborn son . . . and laid him in a manger, because there was no room for them in the inn," provides us with no reason for supposing any bad will on the part of the people of Bethlehem in that they refused to take Joseph and Mary in because they saw how poor they were.

The natural meaning of the text rather leads us to suppose that the holy couple were late in arriving in the town—unquestionably because of Mary's condition, which would preclude hasty travel—and found the caravansary already filled with guests who had likewise come to register in the census. Quite unruffled, and accustomed as he was to the life of poverty, Joseph looks for a cave in the side of the hill on which Bethlehem was built. "The days for her to be delivered were fulfilled. And she brought forth her first-born son" (Luke 2:6) in the cave that Joseph had found, and there it was that the shepherds would come to venerate the new-born Child.

Having decided to extend his stay at Bethlehem, Joseph would have no trouble fixing up the cave as a more comfortable dwelling, so that Matthew (2:1–12) could call it a "house." It would be unusual, then as now, to find houses for sale or rent in the villages. But, as he was an experienced carpenter, Joseph might well have put up a little wall with a door at the entrance of it, thereby transforming the cave into a "house" into which the Magi could come with their gifts of gold, frankincense and myrrh for the Child.

During his public life, our Lord must have been familiar with other poor dwellings like those to be seen nowadays. Most of them are built against the hillsides, which saves building one wall and makes it easier to reach the roof. This is used as much as the inside of the house. It is cooler there on summer nights and provides a place to dry out fruits and grains gathered at the end of summer for winter use. This ready access to the roof also makes it easier, at the beginning of winter, to repair and reinforce the roof itself which is made of packed earth on a framework of tree branches.

Nearby it is usual to dig a cellar in the side of the hill for the storage of ground grain, oil and other supplies. This arrangement which can still be seen today in our villages, helps us to understand some of the gospel texts.

Thus, Luke 11:5-9, tells of the insistent friend. All the details are easily explained when we compare the gospel account with what can be seen in the home of a poor village family nowadays: the sleeping-mats, which are picked up and carefully put aside during the day, are spread out at night in the single room and the whole family sleep on them side by side.

"And he said to them, 'Which of you shall have a friend and shall go to him in the middle of the night and say to him: "Friend, lend me three loaves, for a friend of mine has just come to me from a journey, and I have nothing to set before him"; and he from within should answer and say, "Do not disturb me; the door is now shut, and my children and I are in bed; I cannot get up and give to thee?" I say to you, although he will not get up and give it to him because he is his friend, yet because of his persistence he will get up and give him all he needs.' "

Actually, the only "door was shut," and the master of the house could not "get up to give the three loaves of bread requested by his neighbor" because that would not leave enough for his children. We can take it for granted that he did not insist.

In passing let us note, among other things, the virtues of hospitality, which I shall return to later. The host who receives someone will go through fire to receive him properly. Perhaps he will even deprive himself of his own portion in order to offer it to his visitor, even if it is a simple unknown traveller who has asked shelter. If he has nothing himself to offer, he will knock at his neighbor's door quite naturally, and with insistence if he must. But he will never say to his guest: "I cannot receive you"!

Likewise it is thought completely normal, a "friendly quality," to give one's neighbor everything that he needs to receive his guest worthily.

So it is in Matthew 6:6: "When you pray, go into your room, and closing your door, pray to your Father in secret; and your Father, who sees in secret, will reward you." It is necessary to understand "room" in the sense of cellar, or perhaps the upper room of better-off families, unless we assume that the prayer takes place at a moment when the other members of the family are all outside the single room of the house.

In the scene of the healing of the paralytic Luke (5:19), who speaks of "tiles," is thinking rather of the roof of a Greco-Roman house! Mark, nearer to the Palestinian reality, speaks more exactly: "The four men stripped off the roof above the place where Jesus was . . ." (2:4), that is, they lifted up a part of the packed earth flat roof and its supporting framework of branches. The incident took place in summer, which means that the packed earth was not too tightly packed and the cracks made by the summer's heat made the task undertaken by these four men all the easier.

Reproducing Peter's account as he does, would not Mark recall the dust that the apostles felt dropping on their heads as the men overhead began the unusual manoeuver of making a hole in the roof?

There is another gospel expression that has a familiar ring to our present-day masons, who never build except on a rock foundation, even if they have to dig down quite a distance to find it. Only a "foolish man" will build his house on "sand." It will not be long before his house will develop cracks and begin to collapse (Matthew 7: 24–27). The Arabic translation which speaks of "dust" seems better than English versions that have "sand," since sand is regarded by our masons as a perfectly good foundation.

THE TEMPLE

It is unquestionable that one of the most important buildings known to our Lord was the temple.

Even what remains of it today provides an impressive idea of what it must have been in our Lord's time. As we look at its tremendous foundations, which are still in place, we cannot help but share in the disciples' awe: "Jesus left the temple and was going away when his disciples came forward to show him the buildings of the temple" (Matthew 24:1) and said. "Master, look what wonderful stones and buildings!" (Matthew 13:1). Nor do we experience any difficulty in appreciating the apostles' surprise at the Master's answer: "Do you see all these things? Amen I say to you, there will not be left one stone upon another that will not be thrown down" (Matthew 24:2).

When one looks out at the view of Jerusalem from the top of the Mount of Olives or sees the same scene in a photograph, one's attention is first of all attracted to the broad temple area and the magnificent dome of the Mosque of Omar which dominates it.

This dome is built over the rock where that part of the temple which contains the "Holy Place" and the "Holy of Holies" was built, and which only the priests or the high priest could enter. This was the summit of Mount Moriah, the site, according to a constant tradition, of Abraham's sacrifice and the center of the building operations begun by David and brought to completion by Solomon. Several times destroyed and restored, the building which our Lord knew was the work of Herod the Great, the Idumean, and was more than forty years in building. One of Titus' Roman soldiers set fire to the pile in the year 70 at the time of the fall of the Holy City to the Romans.

The temple is now replaced by the Mosque of Omar, whose cupola and beautiful mosaics are much admired.[6] All around the temple proper extended the "Court of the Jews," to which only men were admitted. Somewhat lower and separated by a number of steps, which are still there, was the "Women's Court," beyond which women were not permitted to go.[7]

Still lower was the Court of the Gentiles, the largest part of the temple area, where Jews and pagans mingled— merchants, money-changers and pilgrims, men and beasts.

This outer court was bordered by rooms similar to those which can be found there today, where the doctors of the

---

6. This is the place from which Mohammed is supposed to have ascended to heaven and is the second most important Moslem holy place, "Thani El Haramein."

7. Unquestionably it was at the limit of this court, beyond which Mary could not go, that Justinian built the magnificent Basilica of the Theotokos, with its five naves, now converted into a mosque south of the "Dome," on the edge of the "Temple area."

Law taught as do the "Ulemas" today, and where the poor pilgrims can find a place of refuge as well.

These four sections were called "the temple," and the evangelists assumed that their readers would understand to which part they had reference.

Our Lord, who did not belong to the priestly caste, never penetrated into the holy place, or the Holy of Holies. He could go only as far as the "Men's Court," (see Acts 21:27–29), where the Jews accused Paul of having brought a gentile into the court reserved to Jews.

Thus it is false to represent the temple as one of our great churches, or even as a spacious synagogue. And with each gospel text it is necessary to try to understand what it denotes. In reading some of the texts, we can fix the exact meaning.

The presentation of Jesus in the temple (Luke 2:22–38) took place in the "Women's Court," where Mary could go. A priest was required to take his station on one of the steps separating the "Men's Court" from the women's. Here he received the price of redemption of the first-born, "a pair of turtledoves or two young pigeons." He would then allow Simeon to receive the infant in his arms. It is there also that the prophetess Anna met the holy family.

However, the house of "Holy Mary, where she was born," over which is built the imposing basilica of St. Anne —traditionally regarded as Mary's birthplace—is not much more than a hundred yards from the temple. The early Christians might well have supposed that she spent the years before her betrothal and life at Nazareth "close by" the temple.

Chapter 2:41–50 of Luke tells of Jesus' first visit to the

temple. He was twelve years old, the age of puberty in the Orient, when a boy took his place in Jewish society and was therefore introduced to the Law's prescriptions. Mary and Joseph, after searching for three days, "found him in the temple, sitting in the midst of the teachers, listening to them and asking them questions" (v. 46). Jesus was there, in a room on the edge of the Court of the Gentiles, where even in our day the *Ulemas* teach the Law (and the Koran).

It was in this court also that the incident of the purification of the temple related in Matthew 21:12 ff. and John 2:13–17 took place, when Jesus expelled the merchants who had turned his Father's house into a market. The "whip of cords" which Jesus used must have been simply the cord he wore as a belt, which, now as then, is used to gather at the waist the long tunic worn by men.

The scene in Luke 21:1–4, wherein Jesus contrasts the offerings of the rich and the widow's mite, took place in the "Men's Court" where Jesus stood surrounded by his disciples. The box for offerings was placed between the two courts, the women's and the men's. From his higher position, our Lord noticed the "poor widow" and, as she went away, he pointed to her and said, "this poor widow has put in more than all."

Likewise, when Luke (19:47) shows us Jesus "teaching daily in the temple," it is in the "Men's Court" that he is doing this.

As for the destruction of the temple prophesied by Jesus, and fulfilled by Titus in 70 A.D. (Mark 13:1–37; Matthew 24:1–51; Luke 21:5–36), it involved the whole temple with all its structures and its porches for the various courts, and included the holy place and the Holy of Holies.

PART II

THE LIFE HE CHOSE

CHAPTER FIVE

CHILDHOOD

In examining the life of our people of today, many details allow us to make useful comparisons, and to come near to ordinary life in the time of our Lord. Modern day observation helps to explain many scriptural texts that at first sight appear difficult to understand.

In order to clarify this point, it will be sufficient to examine the different stages of a man's life: childhood, adolescence, maturity, death. In each stage, there will appear events that are connected with the gospel and are quite ordinary.

PRENATAL DAYS

Traditionally, today, the best greeting one can address to young married couples is: "Befarhet ariss!" (lit. "with the joy of a boy") that is: "May we be able to congratulate you on the birth of a child!"

A sterile woman is a calamity. She will be unhappy and the cause of unhappiness for her family. Wherever divorce is permitted, she very often runs the risk of being cast off; where bigamy is allowed, she risks at least being relegated to second place. The Moslem husband will take a second wife in the hope that she will give him children. Even in Christian families in the villages there are numerous cases

49

where the husband has a concubine, by whom he hopes to have children!

And everyone wants the child to be a boy!

It might almost be said that girls do not count. In the villages the most important family is not always the one that is richest; more usually it is the one with the most boys in it. Such a family will be freely conceded a certain authority in the village, because it has so many "rifles," that is to say, so many sons capable of carrying rifles. Hence the importance of the boy, always preferred to the girl. Until recently, the father who was dividing his fortune would disinherit his daughters completely or leave them, at best, a very small pittance. The Moslem code, still officially in force in many Oriental countries, gives to a boy a portion of the inheritance double that allowed to a girl.

These remarks can clarify one of the gospel texts, without disturbing its messianic import. In Luke 1:19: "The angel answered Zachary, 'I am Gabriel . . . and I have been sent to speak to you and to bring you this good news!' " (i.e., of the birth of a son). It is the birth of a boy that will "take away my [Elizabeth's] reproach among men" (1:25).

BIRTH

News of the birth is announced to all the relatives, who hasten around to offer the customary felicitations. In very distinguished circles, the happy parents offer "moughli," or ground rice highly sweetened and well cooked, which is served in large cups and covered with pistachios or sweet almonds.

But among the Bedouins the birth of a child attracts little more attention than the birth of a kid.

In a caravan, the man mounted on a horse or a camel is little concerned that his wife, who follows on foot, often carries heavy burdens on her shoulders or her head. If she should feel the pangs of childbirth, she withdraws a little way from the caravan, which does not even stop for her. She takes the new-born child, places it on top of the other things she is already carrying, and rejoins the caravan.

Usually, among our people, the mother stays in bed for a few days and it is her neighbors, if she has no relatives, who help her and look after her housekeeping.

These details make it possible for us to understand better the two births, noted in the gospels in very simple words which presume, as always, that the readers are familiar with the customs involved.

(a) The birth of John: "Elizabeth . . . brought forth a son. And her neighbors and kinsfolk heard that the Lord had magnified his mercy towards her, and they rejoiced with her" (Luke 1: 57).

(b) The birth of Jesus: "She brought forth her first-born son"(Luke 2: 7; Matthew 1: 25). Nothing prevents us from supposing that, if Mary's parents were still alive, word was sent to them at Jerusalem and that they hastened to join Mary at Bethlehem. Since the holy family was deprived, by being so far from Nazareth, of relatives, who would come to offer their congratulations, it receives the congratulations of the shepherds, who have been informed by the angels' song (Luke 2:8–21).

NAMES

Before contact was made with the West, family names were unknown in the Orient. To the proper name was added that of the father and of the grandfather: John, son of Peter, son of Paul. Ordinarily, the parents take the name of their eldest son; thus they will be called Abu-Elias (Father of Elias) and Oum-Elias (Mother of Elias). If the first child is a daughter, her parents will not take her name but that of the eldest boy when he comes along.

Usually the father will give his own father's name to his eldest son: Abu-Elias (Father of Elias) is usually himself Son of Elias. The result of this custom, rarely departed from, is that a young man, even before his marriage, will always be called by his friends by the name of his father, which he is expected to give in turn to his son later on. Even if the young man remains single or if he has only daughters, still he will be called by that same name, which he would have given to his son, if he had had one. The son of Elias, then, will be called Abu-Elias, even before his marriage and even if he has, in fact, no son named Elias. This custom predominates in Arab Palestine and in the neighboring countries.

In other Arab countries and among the Hebrews, a man is called "son of . . ." instead of "father of . . ." Thus in Arabia, King Ibn Saud (son of Saud) was called Abd-El-Aziz. The present King is called Saud, Ibn Abd-El-Aziz (son of Abd-El-Aziz). Similarly, in certain North African countries: Ben-Arafa (son of Arafa), Ben-Yussef, Ben-Zvi, Ben-Gurion, etc.

In the gospel we can observe both these tendencies: "Simon, son of Jona" (Matthew 16:17), "James, son of

Zebedee" (Matthew 10:2), and "James, son of Alphaeus" (Matthew 10:3).

On the other hand Mary, after the birth of Jesus, will take her name from that of her son, and will, after the manner of all present-day women, take pride in being called: "Oum-Yashua" (Mother of Jesus). This will be her proper name. Thus, when we encounter the designation "Mother of Jesus" in the account of the marriage at Cana (John 2:1) and in Acts (1:14), we ought perhaps to look on it simply as her proper name.

Names of this sort do not, obviously, exclude the use of some descriptive name-suffix to distinguish its bearer from others of the same name: "Simon called the Zealot" (Luke 6:15) probably to distinguish him from Simon, son of Jona.

As a final point in this sketch on childhood, mention must be made of the large number of children who are an inevitable part of any gathering whatsoever. These children roam the streets of the villages and towns and cities, because their homes are too cramped to hold them. They are today a great cause of disorder at public gatherings and often even in church. If we did not have before us the example of the Savior, drawing them to him, how often we would be tempted to "rebuke" them (Matthew 19:13; Luke 18:15) just as the apostles did.

CHAPTER SIX

ADOLESCENCE

CLANS

Today, as in the old days, the young boy enters officially into the community at the age of twelve—the age of puberty. He will then be admitted into a more exalted circle than that of the children. And because of that very fact, he will have less and less contact with girls. Though little boys and little girls can mix, play together, travel together and the like, these relations become rarer and rarer after the age of puberty. We shall see later just how strictly this principle is observed; it will be the cause of many a death and many a family quarrel.

The young lads, among themselves, call each other "brother." In speaking to a girl, they address her as "sister." To an older person, a younger one will say "uncle" or "aunt," sometimes even "grandfather" or "grandmother." One has only to listen a few minutes to any conversation whatever to hear frequently repeated the words: "Ya akhi" (my brother), "ya ukhti" (my sister), "ya sidi" (my grandfather), "ya sitti" (my grandmother).

Relatives who are at loggerheads among themselves will not show it if a common interest requires their presenting a solid front. The Arab proverb says: "My brother and I will stick together against my cousin; my cousin and I against the outsider" (Anaweiakhi ala ibn amni; ana weibn ammi algharib). Brothers, sisters and cousins make up the clan. If the number of the men is not imposing enough, the sisters and their families will be mentioned; otherwise these latter will not count. Actually, in case of inter-clan strife, the woman will follow her husband's clan, which may easily be in opposition to the clan of her own parents.

It is no doubt in this sense that the texts of Matthew 13:53-58 and Mark 6:1-6 must be understood. The "brothers" mentioned are the cousins who composed the clan to which Jesus belonged, a clan which cannot have been very large, since the need was felt to speak of the "sisters," i.e., the girl-cousins.

How readily we can understand the text of Luke, which plunges us into the human "clan" of Jesus! The people of Nazareth, especially those who were not of his clan, and who had seen him as a child, had doubtless played with him in the narrow streets of their little village. These found it harder than did others to believe in him and to admit that he was the Messiah.

They were too acquainted with the human side of their fellow-townsman to admit all of that divine side which he had deliberately and effectively concealed for thirty years! Not having the heroic faith necessary, they could only treat Jesus as an imposter and want to lead "him to the brow of the hill on which their town was built" (Luke 4:29).

Today, these clans, into which the villagers are divided and which the occupying powers all too often exploit on the time-honored principle of "divide-and-rule," are not all family groupings by any means. Religion, rite and more recently party politics provide other bases for such groupings. At Nazareth, for instance, the town is sharply divided into sections which, apart from some more recent exceptions, are rigidly split one from another. There is the Oriental quarter (hara sharkieh), so called because it is located at the east of the town. It is occupied solely by Moslems. Then there is the Orthodox quarter (haret er-roum) inhabited primarily by the Orthodox, who, in fact, live around their church. Finally, there is the Occidental quarter (haret el-gharbiin) populated mostly by the faithful of the Catholic religion (Melchites, Latins, Maronites) or by Anglicans. It is obviously in this quarter that the various Catholic churches have been built.

In all the other villages where there are different religions, the Christian quarter can be distinguished from the Drusian quarter or the Moslem quarter, and it is only rarely that there is any intermingling.

The customs of different ways of life and of differing mentalities, and often simple prudence, make these religious "clans" necessary.

The struggles between the different "clans" are numerous, and are often touched off by the most trifling causes. In our present-day villages these contests often begin at "the fountain," where discord among the women of different clans arises. An insulted woman will stir up her clan, and truly Homeric struggles can ensue.

It may happen that a member of a somewhat weak clan will seek assistance and refuge from an unrelated clan, even of a different religion (it is "tanib").

The clan that accords its protection to its "guest" will protect him despite any odds against everything, even at the risk of great danger to itself and enmity with its own partisans or co-religionists. This is the law of Arab hospitality, so often extolled. If "aman" (assurance) is granted to anyone, even if he had murdered his father, the pledge given will bind the one who has given it, and he will perform miracles for his protégé.

This does not seem to have been the basis of divergent religions at the time of our Lord. But strife between "sects" is mentioned again and again. The evangelists assume that their readers are familiar with these sects and often content themselves with simply naming them: Pharisees, Saducees, Herodians.

The Pharisees, sometimes hypocrites themselves, and often scornful of the people and scrupulous in all the outward observances of the law, are the ones we meet most often crossing the path of Jesus.

The Saducees, the "free-thinkers" of their day, make one or two attempts to question Jesus, even to put him in a bad light. Jesus, for his part, tries to win them over, to enlighten them (Mark 12:18 ff.). He is not severe with them for they are acting out of weakness, rather than from pride or hypocrisy.

The Herodians, sometimes mentioned together with the Pharisees, are the opportunists, the place-hunters. They despise Jesus, whose influence on the people they fear (Mark 8:15; 12:13).

The gospel hardly ever explains the reasons for the rivalry between the various clan-like sects. A scene in the Acts of the Apostles shows Paul exploiting the opposition between the Pharisees and the Saducees, in order to win his hearers for his cause (Acts 23:6-10).

But what the gospel does mention, almost on every page,

is the strife between Jesus himself and the Pharisees. This strife, though veiled in the first days of Christ's teaching career, soon shows itself as a fight to the death. To the mind of Jesus, no compromise is possible for it is precisely from a warped "Pharisaism" that he has come to save religion and the world. The Pharisees, for their part, see this danger from the first, and wait only the opportune moment to do away with this intruder.

The progressive intensification of this struggle is evident with each succeeding chapter of the Gospel. It is foreshadowed by the Baptist's invectives against this "brood of vipers" (Matthew 3:7). It reaches its climax in the series of eighteen maledictions (Matthew 23) when one would say that the usually kindly Jesus seems unable to control his fury. In the most violent terms he upbraids the hypocritical Pharisees in the hearing of the people who went in fear of them. These maledictions make one shiver, and from them to the cross is but a step.

But it is this step that saved us. What a calamity if our human views reintroduce this kind of Pharisaism into the Church of Jesus, who was crucified to deliver us from it!

WOMEN'S OCCUPATIONS

This subject deserves some attention, for it will enable us to reconstruct the everyday occupations of Mary, the young girl; and later of Mary, "Oum-Yashua" (Mother of Jesus).

A little girl is free to play her favorite games with children her own age. But from the age of eight or nine, a girl who would escape a severe beating must do the work her mother requires of her. The child's first task will be to fetch water from the fountain or well, morning and evening. Even the briefest stroll around Nazareth or any other Arab village will suffice to show, even today, women and girls, cheerfully carrying on their heads pitchers full of water. Sometimes in these post-war years, the pitchers have been replaced by the less esthetic jerry-cans, abandoned by the armies.

After it is fetched the water will be used for washing, cooking, or scouring out the room or the grotto which serves as a dwelling-place. A young girl truly wants to help her mother just as much as she is able.

Once a week she will make the bread ready, the basic food of every villager. This bread is made with admirable art at times. It is delicate as lacework, and nearly twenty inches in diameter. Folded in quarters, it can be kept fresh for several days.

This thin bread will at the same time serve as plate and as spoon. Members of the family and their guests haunch down on the ground or on matting round a low table. On this the common dish is laid: rice or *borgol* (pounded wheat) with some pieces of meat and sour milk. They all eat from the same dish with their fingers, using the bread to convey morsels to the mouth.

The task of weaving garments for the husband and the children falls to the women more than to the young girls. To the extent that the wife is skilful and industrious, peace and prosperity reign in their home. "The man brings home money, but the woman builds it," says an Arab proverb ("Ar-rajoul janna, wel-mara banna").

These various activities occupy the woman from dawn to early in the afternoon. After a short pause following the midday meal, there is another trip to the village fountain, where the women gather in large numbers to chatter and exchange pieces of news—"the evening newspaper." These gatherings are often the occasion for disagreements, insults, and arguments that sometimes assume quite serious dimensions.

Lastly, let us observe that in the villages the women are very early risers. They are up at dawn, and open the gate for the animals who have slept under the same roof with the whole family. To sketch their attire: a long dress that they have sewn themselves, caught in about the waist by a belt of the same material. The hair is brought back from the forehead with a quick movement of both hands and secured under a veil that holds it back all day long. The mattresses or matting are rolled up and put to one side, and the workday begins.

MEN'S OCCUPATIONS

Did our Lord go to school? Were there any schools?

The experience of our villages (before recent progress in education) permits a categorical negative in reply to this question. At Nazareth where our Lord spent his youth, as in all our villages, there was no school.

Our Lord never went to school. And for a very good reason. Mary never went to any school. The education of young girls was something absolutely unknown, and right up until today it was thought of as a luxury that few families could afford their daughter.

Just as today, there were only the courts of religion in former times. Here certain distinguished rabbis held courts of the "Torah" or of the "Talmud" in the buildings connected with the temple. These helped certain fortunate students who desired to devote themselves completely to the study of the "Law and the Prophets." Today as well the sheiks ("ulemas") teach the Koran, and occasionally some rules of Arabic grammar, just outside the most important mosques in certain large cities.

In the time of our Lord lessons such as these were given outside the temple in Jerusalem. But nothing allows us to suppose that Jesus attended any of these. There is only the exceptional three-day period at the age of twelve, noted by Luke (2:41-50), where "all who were listening to him were amazed at his understanding and his answers."

Jesus' countrymen joined with the rest in showing their astonishment. It is this fact that gives us the knowledge that they had never seen him go to school: " 'Where did he get this wisdom?' they said" (Matthew 13:54). A great number who listened to him were amazed, and said: "Where did he get all this? What is this wisdom that is given to him?" (Mark 6:2).

But on the other hand if Jesus never went to school, we can say that he went to the synagogue regularly, on the Sabbath and on the feast days, as does every good Jew. Following a pious tradition, this synagogue of our Lord for many years has been the parish church at Nazareth. Today it is the only holy place that belongs to both the Greek and the Melkite community, and is venerated by both.

Ordinarily a boy is given the task of grazing the flocks. He usually leads them off to "the mountain," an extensive area covered over with bushes at the end of summer and with wild grass after the winter rains. It is a rare village that does not have some stony land held in common where the flocks graze ("Ahrache").

It is there that the young shepherds spend the day and eat the frugal meal that their mothers put up for them when they left at dawn: bread, some olives, an onion. A little before the sun sets they start back on the return trip. They try to pause near a well or a spring so that their animals can drink.

Nothing prevents us from thinking that our Lord tended his father's goats or sheep, if Joseph was sufficiently well-off to buy any. At any rate, he seems to speak as one who knows when he is telling in detail of the relationship between sheep and shepherd (John 10:1-18): "I am the good shepherd. The good shepherd lays down his life for his sheep. But the hireling . . . sees the wolf coming and leaves the sheep and flees . . . I know mine and mine know me . . ."

From the time he is eighteen, the young man begins hard work in the fields, hard that is, at certain periods: seeding after the first rains, harvesting after Pentecost. During the winter months the men have much more leisure and spend their time in social groups, sipping coffee and chatting—while the women go on working with no respite.

CHAPTER SEVEN

BETROTHAL

At this point, more than anywhere else, it is absolutely necessary to get rid of all Western ideas about courtship and marriage, if we wish to understand the gospel texts at all. The marriage customs of the East persist to this day, in undiminished vigor, in spite of their flat contradiction of modern ways of thinking and, sometimes, even of the teachings of the Church herself.

AGE

Boys and girls are promised in marriage very young. Usually when the girl is twelve or thirteen; the boy fifteen or sixteen. Neither has anything to say about the choice of his or her life partner. Everything is arranged by the parents, often as soon as the children are born. When the relatives gather to congratulate the mother, who has just had a baby, match-making begins. This little girl will be for so-and-so, some relative of hers, born three or four years before. And often the two families exchange a promise, which they will make it a point of honor to respect when the time comes.

In very many cases the bridal pair see each other for the first time at the moment of the wedding ceremony. The parents will have arranged everything and it simply does

5

not occur to the young couple to raise the least objection.

Furthermore, at the moment of the betrothal nobody worries much about the future. If, later on, the husband is out of work, the wife will help him out by working herself. The vital thing for any man, at the moment of the betrothal, is to be able to offer his fiancée the traditional gift: bottles of perfume or eau de cologne—strongly scented and vividly colored—along with a few jewels. During the betrothal, the fiancé must be able to purchase a wardrobe with mirrors and present to his bride-to-be the materials with which she will make her trousseau and her dresses.

Among the Moslems, the fiancé, who is, in fact, depriving his father-in-law of a valuable helping hand, must indemnify him by paying the "mohr," a sort of dowry fixed according to the family's wealth and often paid in two installments.

On the basis of these customs, one will probably not be far wrong in concluding that Joseph was about sixteen when he was betrothed to Mary, who was then about thirteen. Married at fourteen, the "Mother of Jesus" would thus have been widowed at forty-four or forty-five.

FIDELITY

Betrothal is a bond which is not easy to break. Ecclesiastical betrothal, when it takes place, can be set aside only by a sentence of the ecclesiastical tribunal. Custom dictates that a man who breaks his engagement without grave cause must leave his fiancée all the jewels and other gifts he has given her.

Incidentally, there is no reason whatever to think that there are any liberties or improper relations between engaged couples in the genuine Oriental atmosphere. Such liberties which are frequently taken in Western families or by those natives who have adopted Western ways, are unknown among the simple villagers. The most that can happen is that the betrothed couple may meet once every two or three months in the presence of a great many witnesses. Much less should it ever be thought that engaged couples might live together under the same roof. That would be an impossible breach of convention in the East.

All this has its basis in that respect for woman, from this point of view, which is common to Oriental, Moslem and Christian alike.

Hardly a month goes by without headlines about some girl who has been murdered by her brother or her cousin for having had illicit relations. Very often the guilty man is killed together with her or will be killed later. I have several times had to be the horrified witness of scenes in which a whole delegation of Christians came to announce to us triumphantly that so-and-so had finally killed his sister who had been betraying the family honor, which he had redeemed by bloodshed.

Local custom permits that a woman, violated against her will, i.e., if she has called for help (sarkha), may sometimes be spared. But if she is a consenting party (radiah), it is rare that she gets off. Such infamies are blotted out only by blood! Her murderer very often gives himself up to the police who will not fail to take into account this extenuating circumstance.

These customs find their echo in the Old Testament and, at least on two occasions, the gospel alludes to them: the adulteress brought to Jesus, to be stoned according to the law of Moses, is pardoned to the great scandal of certain Eastern Fathers, who denied the authenticity of the passage (John 8:1-12). The other allusion is more touching still, for it has to do with Joseph and Mary (Matthew 1:18). It will be dealt with at the end of this chapter, where an attempt will be made to apply to the holy family all the details mentioned above.

MARRIAGE OF COUSINS

One persistent practice, which is difficult to root out of Oriental families, even Christian ones, despite all the Church's rulings, is the marriage of close relatives. The cousin has priority over all other suitors and his cousin cannot marry another without his consent. A man will sometimes keep his cousin waiting several years and may even prevent her from ever marrying.

I knew of a case where a girl, with the full consent of her family, tried to betroth herself to another suitor over her cousin's refusal to consent. Just as the procession was proceeding to the church for the nuptial blessing, the cousin and his "clan" tried to kill the rash bridegroom. They missed him but killed three other people. The wedding was turned into a multiple funeral!

And I know of numerous cases where the cousin, himself unable for one reason or another to marry, makes his cousin wait. Sometimes she does not love her cousin and would like to marry the man of her choice. Our attempts at intervention do not always succeed and the parents' reply often runs something like this: "Our daughter is not the sort to have a mind of her own" or even, "My daughter must obey me! I know what's best for her better than she does."

Crying injustices, these, grounded on the inferior position in which the Oriental woman is still confined. Such a state of affairs will continue for a long time to come.

JOSEPH AND MARY

After all these details, an attempt may be made to understand the betrothal of Joseph and Mary, to which the gospel makes only vague references.

The charming story of the flowering staff of the aged Joseph, which is the sign predestining him, in the eyes of the high priest, to be the spouse of a Mary who is living piously in the temple, has no foundation whatever in fact. It colored the ideas of our earliest childhood and continues to inspire those artists who depict an aged Joseph, holding a flowering staff and the Christ child in his arms.

In point of fact Mary was not at the temple; she could not be there for the simple reason that there was no place there for her. And the high priest had nothing to do with her marriage.

The reality seems to have been much simpler. Mary, born at Jerusalem, must have been promised from birth to her cousin, Joseph. When she was thirteen or fourteen and Joseph was sixteen or seventeen, the two families decided that the young couple should be betrothed. The betrothal feast must have taken place at Jerusalem, assuming that Mary's parents were still alive. Otherwise, Mary would perhaps have been taken in at the death of her father by the family of her sister "Mary of Cleophas" (John 19:25) in Nazareth and then it would be there that the betrothal took place. This second supposition fits better the course of events and is more in line with the Protoevangelium of James, which mentions—for what it is worth—the advanced age of Joachim and Anna, at the time of Mary's miraculous birth.

Mary, then, was at Nazareth, not at the home of her fiancé, Joseph. She was at her sister's place or in the home of some other member of the family, where she receives the "Annunciation" that she is chosen to be the mother of the "Messiah," and hears the angel's greeting: "Hail, full of grace! The Lord is with thee!" (Luke 1:26-28).

The annunciation at Nazareth takes place after the betrothal, because the gospel explicitly notes here (Luke 1:26-27): "The angel Gabriel was sent from God to a town in Galilee called Nazareth, to a virgin betrothed to a man named Joseph, of the house of David, and the virgin's name was Mary."

It may reasonably be supposed that Mary confided to her cousin Joseph on the day of her betrothal her resolution to "remain a virgin." Joseph, ignorant of what was to come, must have been very much puzzled.

After the Annunciation, Mary "went with haste to go into the hill country, to a town of Juda" (Luke 1:39), undoubtedly to Ain-Karim, to visit her cousin, Elizabeth. When she left Nazareth, a few weeks after her betrothal and a few days after the annunciation, there were no outward signs to betray her condition.

But on her return to Nazareth, three months later, she still did not come to live with Joseph—"before they came together," Matthew will say (1:18)—but went to stay with relatives; a careful observer might well have doubts. Joseph, who would see her sometimes going to the well, was the first to notice the change in his fiancée. That resolve of hers "to remain a virgin," which he had heard from her own lips, all of a sudden seemed to make no sense at all. Moments of torture—days of anguish for this upright soul, rudely plunged into a mystery.

Finally he makes a decision: "not wishing to expose her" as custom would ordinarily dictate he "was minded to put her away privately" (Matthew 1:19), to return her to her own, who would decide what must be done. His decision is taken. His doubts are quieted and his peace of mind returns.

It is then that the Lord came into his life to turn it entirely upside down! A dream explains to him what had up to then been hidden from him: "For that which is begotten in her is of the Holy Spirit" (Matthew 1 : 20). Joseph believes and accepts the role assigned to him: to take Mary under his protection and to give his name to the child.

The very next day, Joseph, instead of repudiating his fiancée, tells Mary's relatives of his decision to advance the date of the marriage. The festivities take place before the prying and curious eyes of outsiders have any grounds for suspecting her. It is only then, after the official marriage, that Joseph took his wife into his home (Matthew 1: 24). "And he did not know her" during the four or five months that follow "till she brought forth her first-born son. And he called his name Jesus."

In the little hamlet of Nazareth, where some at least would not have forgotten the date of the marriage, the birth of the child after four or five months could not have failed to make some tongues wag.

As a measure of prudence, Joseph, obliged to go "to the town of David, which is called Bethlehem" to register (Luke 2:3-4) takes along Mary "who was with child." Neither the story nor Oriental customs give any grounds for supposing that the registration was equally binding on women. Mary might well have been excused from making such a long journey in her condition. But at Bethlehem, far from prying eyes, the "premature" birth of the child had every chance of going unnoticed.

When the holy family returns to Nazareth, some years later, people will have had time to forget—if there were any need—the shortness of the interval between Joseph's marriage and Jesus' birth.

CHAPTER EIGHT

MARRIAGE

Today, as in centuries past, a wedding in the East is characterized by a round of celebrations, lasting three days, sometimes even seven days before the marriage (cf. Judges 14:10, 12, 17). These celebrations conclude for the Christian villagers with the nuptial blessing in the church; for the Moslems with the bringing of the bride to her husband's house. The gospel alludes to these ceremonies repeatedly, and it is important to a clear understanding of the text to know what is involved in them, although due to Muslim influence they have been somewhat modified since biblical times.

We shall link our exposition to the pertinent gospel texts as we go along. The marriage at Cana, mentioned by St. John, Chapter 2, deserves a special explanation; we shall treat it therefore separately and at greater length.

THE "FRIEND OF THE BRIDEGROOM"

The essential part of the wedding festivities is the marriage feast. The rhythm of the tambourines, the measured beat of the popular songs, the clever improvisations of the professional "poets"—all these are only added attractions.

During the betrothal period, the bridegroom will save

up what he needs for the feast (or feasts!): mutton or goatsmeat, dried fruits, olives, borgol (wheat-meal) and rice. Some fresh vegetables will be bought just before the feast. Drinks are also carefully provided in advance—nowadays arak (spiced spirits) or beer, formerly, wine. Everything is stored at the back of the living-room or in a special cave nearby (natural refrigeration).

The bridegroom, who is very busy at the time of the marriage—for reasons we shall explain later—must choose in advance a substitute to whom he will entrust the management of all the material arrangements of the wedding. He will not ordinarily be a member of the family (father or brother) but more likely a cousin or a close friend. The bridegroom will brief this friend on just what stores are available, tell him exactly everything he has. Indeed, if the bridegroom were to conceal anything from his chosen deputy, he would be violating the most elementary rules of friendship.

This "friend of the bridegroom" will receive the guests, offer them food and drinks, and will be responsible in the eyes of all for the practical organization of the banquets. If anything begins to run short, he, not the bridegroom, will have to remedy the situation. If everything goes off to perfection, the "friend of the bridegroom" will feel a greater personal satisfaction than if it had been his own party. He will not have disappointed the trust placed in him; he will be happy to be his friend's sponsor on the wedding day and to remain in the background thereafter in order to leave the newlyweds to their new-found happiness.

In a delightful metaphor, reported by John (3:30), John

the Baptist compares himself to the "friend of the bridegroom"— the latter being his cousin, Jesus—who "rejoices
exceedingly at the voice of the bridegroom." And quite
naturally he adds: "He must increase, but I must decrease."

The man whom John, in his description of the wedding
at Cana calls the "master of the feast" and whom some
translators call the "steward" or even the "maître d'hotel"
is none other than the "friend of the bridegroom" whose
role we have just been explaining in detail.

WEDDING SEASON

Lent is liturgically a closed season, during which the
nuptial blessing is not given. Even if it were not for this
prohibition, the villagers would not choose this time of
year: Lent falls in the dead of winter, and one just does not
get married then.

The normal wedding season is summer, for the simple
reason that during the rainy season it is impossible even to
think of wedding celebrations. The average dwelling-place,
be it room or cave, does not lend itself to such celebrations.
The gatherings, the songs, the music, the tambourines—all
belong outside the house or on the roof, which is reserved
for certain favored guests. In organizing these celebrations,
one must be sure that it will not rain. And that is why
weddings are usually held between May and October. Only
by way of exceptional necessity will a wedding be held
between November and April, and usually such a wedding
will be a very simple affair.

During the summer days, the heat being quite extreme,
particularly where shade-trees are few and far between,

the celebrations have to wait till sunset to begin. In point of fact the social gatherings that precede a wedding always take place in the evening and sometimes last till late into the night. The danger of disturbing the neighbors is lessened by the fact that the entire neighborhood takes part in the festivities!

We must assume, then, that the majority of the wedding feasts which Jesus attended or of which he speaks took place in the evening, even if the gospel does not note it explicitly. On one occasion, however, this fact is indicated in the parable of the wise and foolish virgins (Matthew 25:1-8): the bridegroom appears at midnight and only those bridesmaids who had had the foresight to take along a reserve of oil are admitted to the marriage feast.

Quite often nowadays, too, I relive this long wait, during which everybody becomes drowsy. When I am invited to give the nuptial blessing it is not unusual for me to have to wait a long time for the bridegroom to finish the procession, on which his friends have insisted, through the streets of his village.

What means of illumination was there for all this crowd, sometimes quite a dense one? The gospel mentions oil lamps of which numerous specimens of various kinds have been found in Palestine. They could not have given a very bright light. So it is a logical supposition that, in the old days as now, the people would most likely choose those nights when the moon gave enough light for the banquet areas, especially in summer when the sky in the East is so beautifully clear. The lamps would be used only to light the one room where the banquet was laid out and where the guests would come in a steady stream for refreshments.

THE WEDDING PROCESSION

The preliminary wedding-eve festivities we have just been describing are usually climaxed by the wedding procession, in which Christian bride and bridegroom are escorted to the church for the nuptial blessing, while the non-Christian bride is escorted to her husband's house. This procession is so hedged about with prescribed formalities that both bride and bridegroom are literally the slaves of their friends, and the bridegroom does not have a free moment to look after his guests. This is why he chooses a "friend" to discharge the duties of host in his stead.

On the morning of his wedding day, the unresisting bridegroom—well aware that any resistance would be pointless—is escorted by his close friends to the well where he is given the complete treatment—not unwelcome after the recent nights of dancing, eating and drinking. He is shaved in a special ceremony, to the accompaniment of singing, then lavishly perfumed and decked out in all his finery. Even in the villages, the European type suit is beginning to replace the handsome Oriental "coftan"— a long robe open down the front and fastened by a special button at the left side. But whether he puts on a European suit or a "coftan," the bridegroom always wears on his head the "hatta" or long white veil which covers the head and falls over the shoulders. This veil is held securely in place by the black or gold "igal," an ample hoop made of camel's hair or gold thread. If the village is fairly well off, the bridegroom will be mounted on a fine horse, led by two of his closest friends. If not, these friends will take the bridegroom, one by each arm—and the procession begins.

All these preliminaries take hours, and when they are finished a messenger is dispatched to the young men of the village, who come to escort the bridegroom. They will all walk before him, singing and dancing, beating time with their hands to a rhythm all their own; and will arrive, exhausted and bathed in sweat at the end of the route. The procession winds through every street of the village, stopping before the homes of certain village dignitaries, who consider it an honor to offer the merrymakers a drink or a sweet.

Meanwhile, girls or young women—the older women being busy preparing the food and drink—go to the bride's house. During the preceding three or four days, she has been sitting there enthroned as a queen in the midst of a display of her dresses and the gifts she has received. She is seated in a raised armchair (samde) in the middle of the room, and remains thus "on display" while everyone sings round her and admires her or her presents. When the time comes, she is brought down from her "throne," dressed in her long wedding veil, drenched in perfume[8] and led in procession through the village streets. In the conservative Moslem villages, even the Christian bride has her face covered by a thick veil, which she will not remove even in church, but only when she has been brought into her husband's house, where there are no strangers to stare. The bride's procession, like that of the groom, is accompanied

---

8. A custom still widely observed in some villages decrees that the hands and feet of the bride and of all her young female relatives, even the tiniest children included, be smeared with "henna," a sort of reddish ointment which does not wear off for many a week.

by rhythmic chants, the women clapping their hands and repeating the traditional good wishes they have so often heard sung.

The wife will obey her husband, whom she looks on as her master. In her eyes St. Paul's words fit her husband exactly. She will usually call her husband "ya sidi" (my master) and he will call her "ya binti" (my daughter). When speaking of his wife to a stranger, he will call her "bint' ammi" (my father-in-law's daughter).

WEDDING AT CANA

A great deal has been written about the marriage feast at Cana. Possibly with the result that the quite simple reality, which we still see in any of our villages, has been somewhat obscured.

Certain medieval or renaissance artists, though they have produced undeniable artistic masterpieces, have often done their share to distort this famous gospel scene.

We must stop to consider at some length John's text (2:1-12), every phrase of which, if taken in its obvious meaning, is remarkably precise.

"A wedding took place at Cana in Galilee": let us suppose that this village of Cana was the present-day Kafr-Kanna, a few miles northeast of Nazareth on the road to Tiberias and the lake. It is today a quite important village, numbering about a thousand Christians of all denominations, and close to two thousand Moslems. Coming in from Nazareth, our attention will be attracted by the spring of Cana, because of the large number of women and girls who are there, filling their earthenware pitchers or canteens, which they soon carry away gracefully on their heads. Sixty yards or so further on is the Greek Catholic Church and at some two hundred yards the Latin Church and the Orthodox Church; all these commemorate the marriage feast at which our Lord was present.

No doubt our Lord took part in all the festivities of this wedding, as did all his male relatives. He enjoyed the songs, drank of the wine, took part in the conversation, without anything attracting attention to him—until he performs the miracle, which only the "waiters" will notice. He attended the celebrations with good grace and in all simplicity, wishing, as our prayers put it, "to sanctify marriage by his presence at Cana of Galilee."

"The Mother of Jesus was there." I mentioned before that "Mother of Jesus" had doubtless been Mary's proper name, since she had given birth to her first-born son. Like all present-day mothers, she bears the name of her son: "Oum-Yashua."

"The Mother of Jesus was there": a highly significant detail of the gospel text. She was there, without having received a special invitation. The implication is that she was a relative. The point is that at such a time as a wedding feast a single woman is not enough. Traditionally all the womenfolk who are relatives pitch in, as they are needed, and help one another to prepare food and drinks.

The fact that she is a relative will likewise explain perfectly the liberty she takes later on, especially in giving instructions to the cousins who were serving the wine.

"Now Jesus too was invited to the marriage and also his

A Carpenter

An Arab Meal

Young Shepherd

The Lake of Tiberias (The Lake of Genesareth)

disciples."[9] The reason: Jesus had been gone for some time far from his home village but his relatives in Cana had learned that he was moving all about the country and had attracted some disciples. Was not their fellow-townsman, Nathaniel, one of the group?

If Jesus was invited, he would have to be invited with "his disciples," for convention is very strict on this point. Besides, during these celebrations, the restrictions imposed by Western ways are disregarded. There is always room for a few extra guests. As the banquets take place outside, often on the main highways, passers-by often stop in on them; they will be invited to stay, will be served generously and then go on their way.

The banquet preparations always take into account these last minute guests and, if the host is sometimes caught unawares, he will do all in his power, and then some, to keep the guests from noticing that they are a source of embarrassment. How many times during the war years when food rationing was in force have we not seen a family giving passersby their entire month's meat ration, taking it away from their own children in order to do honor to the guest?

"The wine having run short": very probably too many people had come all at once. No doubt Jesus had come with more disciples than were expected, and Nathaniel must have told his friends on the way that the "rabbi" of whom he had spoken was there, and that they could come and see

---

9. If Joseph had still been alive there is no doubt but that he would have been invited, and the evangelist would not have failed to mention his presence. This omission has given rise to the belief that Joseph was dead before the beginning of Jesus' public life.

him. The very same sort of thing might happen today; a guest would not hesitate to bring several others along with him.

As it was evening, there was no way of getting wine elsewhere, and the hosts would have been very mortified at not being able to take care of all the guests. "Oum-Yashua" was among the women working in the place used as a kitchen for the preparation of everything to be served to the men outside—no public mixing of men and women! She must have heard the cries of distress and sensed the embarrassment of her relatives. No doubt she heard one or other of the women saying that Jesus himself was responsible since he had brought so many people along with him.

Meanwhile, Jesus, humanly speaking, was completely unaware of all these details. Busy teaching or enlightening his listeners, busy, too, listening to the songs and stories, he was unaware of the anxiety his hosts were experiencing.

His mother lets him know tactfully. "The Mother of Jesus said to him: 'They have no wine.' " A young girl would never have dared to come into the midst of the men to speak in public to one of them. But Mary, already almost fifty years old, could take the liberty of coming and whispering a few words in her son's ear. It will be noted, in passing, that the first meeting of Jesus and his Mother since the beginning of his public life takes place at this ceremony. And Mary's first concern is for others, her first request to her son is not for himself: charity, concern for her neighbor, a desire to come to their aid.

"What wouldst thou have me do, woman?" This text which we follow is preferable to the older translations, which carried: "Woman, what is that to me and to thee?";

a rude reply, at first glance, which is offensive to Christian sensibilities and which exegetes have tried, more or less happily, to explain. Some translators, embarrassed by the form of address "woman" have quite simply replaced it by "mother."

And yet, in the eyes of Orientals, the text is so simple. Jesus must have said what a loving and respectful son would say even today to his mother: "malesh! ya mara": "woman, let's wait and see!" The word "malesh" is a contraction of "ma fi aleiki chi," literally "there is nothing on you." It has its Hebrew counterpart: "Ein-davar" which can also mean "It's nothing. Let's wait and see."

We do not doubt that Jesus, speaking Aramaic, used a similar expression, one not in the least scornful but which aimed simply at quieting the anxiety which the son had noticed on his mother's face.[10]

As to the form of address "woman," we maintain, judging by our present-day usage, that Jesus could not have used

---

[10]. On this point we are happy to follow the great Père Lagrange. Here is what he says in his *Evangile selon St. Jean* (Gabalda, Paris, 1927, p. 56): "The Arabs of Palestine even nowadays frequently say 'ma-lesh.' It is a word whose meaning depends entirely on the tone of voice. Sometimes it means: 'Mind your own business' and sometimes, with a smile, 'Leave it to me. Everything will be all right.'"
Now the whole story attests to the fact that it was in this second way that it was said at Cana, with more dignity in the tone but undoubtedly with more affection in the inflection. A few sentences further on, Lagrange continues: "What is clear is that this first part of the sentence turns down the suggestion made. A refusal can have the overtone of a reproach if the request is really inopportune. That is not the case here, because the reason for the refusal will be of a nature to soften its sternness." In the Old Testament, this Semitism occurs frequently: Judges 11:12; 2 Sam 16:10; 3 Kings 17:18.

any other term. He could not have said "mother" because the Oriental avoids using in public any term implying kinship with a woman, just as he avoids all familiarity. When a husband speaks of his wife he calls her "bint' ammi" (daughter of my father-in-law), an Arab word that can stand equally well for cousin.

One has only to listen briefly to villagers talking in order to hear the words "ya mara" or "ya hurme": "woman." This is the way a husband calls his wife to ask her for something; he would never dream of calling her by her name. This word "mara" is also sometimes used with a sense of endearment. The wife often feels flattered by it. There is, then, nothing shocking in this very simple reply of Jesus to his mother: "woman, 'malesh': let us wait and see!" I do not want to make known just yet who I am.

"His mother said to the attendants: 'Do whatever he tells you.' " In the villages, household servants are unknown and we must certainly not picture to ourselves, at this point, liveried waiters, each with a napkin over his arm. They were the bridegroom's cousins or friends, who are serving drinks to the guests under the direction of the "friend of the bridegroom." The fact that these people obey Mary at once substantiates what we have just said about Mary not being an outsider merely invited in for the occasion but rather a relative, who is entirely at ease in talking to her own cousins, by whom she is unhesitatingly obeyed.

"Now six stone water jars were placed there, after the Jewish manner of purification." Such jars, of various sizes, are still used in the villages. Since running water is unknown, water carried from the cistern or spring is kept in them. These jars are made today of a special potter's clay, which cools the water. Since it is rather rare to find six large jars in a single house, the "friend of the bridegroom" had probably borrowed jars from the neighbors, a practice still common among neighbors who readily lend utensils or kitchenware.

The "Jewish manner of purification," reported in greater detail in Mark, consisted chiefly in a thorough washing of the arms, up to the elbows. Pious Moslems can still be seen performing these ablutions in the street several times a day.

"Jesus said to them [the attendants]: 'Fill the jars with water.' " Such an order cannot have pleased the cousins and friends who were serving, and who might reasonably suppose that Jesus was asking for still more water because he was expecting still more disciples. The situation was bad enough as it was. And so we see the importance of the directions Mary had given them: "Do whatever he tells you."

"And they filled them up to the brim." This must have taken some little time. The water had to be fetched from the nearby spring in smaller containers and then poured into the stone jars, round which Jesus and his disciples were standing. These latter must have seen with their own eyes that it was clear water that was being poured from one vessel into the other.

"And Jesus said to him, 'Draw out now, and take to the chief steward,' " i.e., to the "friend of the bridegroom,"

whose role and importance we have already noted. Jesus
knew well what he was asking, for it would have been a
waste of time to send these servers to the bridegroom
himself, who would have understood nothing of the miracle.

"And they took it to him. Now when the chief steward
had tasted the water after it had become wine, not knowing
whence it was (though the attendants who had drawn the
water knew), the chief steward called the bridegroom, and
said to him: 'Every man at first sets forth the good wine,
and when they have drunk freely, then that which is poorer.
But thou hast kept the good wine until now!' "

Let us try to reconstruct the scene in order to grasp all
the details. It must first be supposed that Mary was not the
only one to notice that "the wine had run short." Some of
the other women would have noticed it as well and one or
the other would have hurried to warn the "friend of the
bridegroom" who was responsible for the general organization, while Mary went to appeal to her son's power.

The immediate result would be that the "friend of the
bridegroom" would be upset, would take measures, no
doubt sending word to the neighbors. Perhaps he even
went himself to look elsewhere for the wherewithal to
honor the too numerous guests, brought by Jesus.

Meanwhile, Jesus had had the stone jars filled and had
changed this water, fresh from the well, into choice wine.
The attendants who offered it to the "friend of the bridegroom" were not the same ones whom the latter had sent
out to try to find wine. These would not yet have had time
to get back. The "friend of the bridegroom" does not ask
them where they got this good wine. Knowing very well

where it had come from, for they had drawn off the "water" themselves, these attendants would have explained everything to him—and the miracle would have been revealed a few moments too soon. The "friend of the bridegroom" naturally thinks that the bridegroom has shown a lack of confidence in him, by keeping from him a special store, where he had hidden his best wine. Thus, he called him— but a little too quickly. The bridegroom was inside, in the one room where the refreshments are offered to the guests, who follow one another in a constant stream as soon as a place is free. Normally this room would hold only a few people. Most of the guests would stay outdoors, drinking, singing and dancing.

The bridegroom, unceremoniously summoned and up-braided point-blank by his friend, simply does not understand his annoyance. He has concealed nothing from his friend, swears to him that he has not been lacking in confidence in him. All this gradually calms the furious friend. It is obvious that the bridegroom knows nothing of "good wine" and the "poorer sort." Both call their cousins, the attendants who had drawn the water, and ask them to explain. These waiters tell all and the miracle is revealed.

But meanwhile, Jesus is no longer there. During the spirited exchange between the bridegroom and his friend, he must have left the scene, accompanied by his disciples, and departed from Cana of Galilee.

The time had not yet come for him to present himself to the general public. It was enough for him, for the moment, to strengthen his disciples' faith. The gospel, in bringing to a close this scene, where all the details are so vividly set down, says this in so many words: "He manifested his glory, and his disciples believed in him."

"After this," continues John, "he went down to Capharnaum" (John 2:12).

As we follow him, a little longer pause on the banks of the lake will provide food for meditation.

CHAPTER NINE

THE LAKE OF TIBERIAS AND TABOR

On the way into Nazareth (about one thousand three hundred feet above sea-level) via the old carriage route, where the vehicles roll at an all too rapid rate down towards Tiberias, the traveller ought to stop at the point where the steep slope begins; all of a sudden, there appear the resplendent blue waters of the lake, set between the mountains of Galilee on the west and those of Syria on the east. Almost the entire public life of our Lord is brought to mind.

Tourists, with too little time at their disposal, spend an hour or two beside the lake, stopping a few moments on its shores at Capharnaum and at "Heptapegon," i.e., "the Seven Springs," where the remains of a Byzantine Church of the Multiplication of the Loaves can still be seen; then, a little higher up, at the "Beatitudes," they will admire, in the lovely little chapel with its walls of glass, the panorama of the lake and the nearby mountains. Pilgrims certainly ought to make a longer stop here.

If you have the good fortune to make a pilgrimage to the Holy Land, be sure not to miss the opportunity of spending a night at the hospice of the Mount of the Beatitudes. You will never forget the evening on the shore of the lake—spent reading the gospel texts, recalling to your mind the scenes which you will feel you see taking place before your very eyes. This and the morning prayer and communion will unquestionably be the most unforgettable memory of your pilgrimage; it will leave a permanent mark on your life as a Christian—and may well transform it.

Let us, therefore, try to savor together the irresistible charm of the Lake of Tiberias, called also in the gospels the Lake of Genesareth, and by the pre-exilic Hebrews, "Sea of Chenereth," because of an old site (present-day Tel-el-Oreimeh) whose name meant "a harp." This has sometimes given rise to the notion that the lake is harp-shaped. (Cf. Dt 3:17; Jos 11:2; Nm 34:11; Jos 12:3; 13:27.)

BEAUTY

There is no doubt that the region about the lake is one of the most beautiful in Palestine, perhaps even in the world. The color contrast, especially on one of those clear days, so frequent in the East, the wild mountains bordering the blue waters, the reflections of the sun's rays on the lake, the little boats slipping through the calm waters whose wavelets gently lap the shore—all these are so many tangible delights to charm the eye, ever eager for more. You can scarcely tear yourself away. You stay for hours, contemplating the enchanting spectacle.

But, to these natural beauties, there is added, for the Christian, a deep emotional attraction: this landscape has not changed down through the centuries and the Master's glance fell upon exactly what we see, except that he knew the proud cities of Capharnaum, Bethsaida, and Corozain. There come to mind the terrible prophecies of doom uttered by our Lord: "Then he began to reproach the towns in which most of his miracles were worked, because they had not repented. 'Woe to thee, Corozain! Woe to thee, Bethsaida! . . . And thou, Capharnaum, shalt thou be exalted to heaven? Thou shalt be thrust down to hell!' " (Matthew 11:20-21, 22). The same sentiments are echoed in Luke 10:13-15.

Perhaps we shall have the opportunity to eat the fish, fresh from the lake, sometimes called "St. Peter's fish," a delicious kind of carp the size of a man's hand, which are caught in large numbers at certain times of the year and in certain parts of the lake well known to fishermen. Nowadays, modern fishing methods tend to replace the nets, formerly so popular, and which we can still admire at our leisure in the Bay of Tyre, in Lebanon.

While we enjoy the "St. Peter's fish," we relive in spirit the first miraculous draught of fishes, recorded in Luke (5:4-11). How clearly we sense here, in Peter, that Oriental courtesy which is always at pains not to hurt the guest's feelings. Jesus was Simon Peter's guest, having entered "one of the boats, the one that was Simon's." After he had preached, he tells Simon to lower his nets "for a catch." Simon could have turned a deaf ear to this request, certain that he knew more about his trade than this stranger guest. But he does not want to offend him; and he tried again, although he certainly needed a rest after having worked all night. He tells him courteously: "but at thy word, I will lower the nets."

It was no small operation; to let down these nets with their heavy lead weights which hold them in the water requires all one's strength. It calls for skill and effort, and is exhausting. Simon's effort is soon rewarded: "They enclosed a great number of fishes," so that the two boats could hardly hold them. Nowadays this is more than a month's catch and would weigh from four to five hundred pounds.

Peter and his three companions, terrified at first by this opening encounter with the supernatural, willingly responded to Jesus' call and "they left all and followed him."

When we see these intrepid fishermen of today, bronzed by the sun, their muscles hardened, their bare arms and legs chapped by constant contact with sun and water—men of lively intelligence no doubt but with so little formal education—the thought that it was men like these who travelled the whole world and founded the Church gives us pause. "Fishers of men," they had Christ in their hearts and at their side.

STORM

If we arrive at the lake in the early morning hours, we shall be struck by the smoothness of its blue waters: a mirror-like surface, scarcely rippled by the gentle wavelets that will softly lap at our feet as we try to drink from our cupped hands, while standing on the shore.

But we should not let ourselves be deceived by this calm. The winds which come up on certain days, especially toward evening, and which, crossing the deep valleys hollowed out in the mountains of the west, break as whirlwinds over the lake, change it all of a sudden into a raging sea. The best thing is just not to be around when this happens.

Our fishermen know this full well. But they know, too, how to escape storms, by heeding the familiar warning signs. These storms can sometimes be foreseen a whole day before they break. The fishermen claim they feel a peculiar vibration in the air, coming, they say, from Ras-el-Naqura. This "Ras" (cape), located on the Mediterranean between Acre and Tyre, and today the border between Palestine on the south and Lebanon on the north, means literally "Battery Cape," the mightily battered headland.

A storm coming from the west first of all strikes Ras-el-Naqura, whose jagged rocks tower over the sea. It will hit the lake of Tiberias twenty-four hours later. It seems to take a whole day to cross these thirty-six miles separating the Mediterranean and the Lake of Genesareth.

But a visitor can scarcely be expected to know these local conditions and, if he is not advised by experienced natives, can find himself in serious difficulties.

This is what happened to our Lord. Let us pause over each detail as we re-read the gospel texts which describe the stilling of the storm, and of Jesus walking on the waves.

In both scenes, the gospel notes that it was evening: "When evening had come" (Mark 4:35); "and when it was late" (Mark 5:47); after the multiplication of the loaves "when the day was far spent" (Mark 6:35).

At this time of day the apostles, well aware of the fickle moods of the lake, would never have risked sailing on it. If they do so on these two particular nights, it is in violation of their instincts and solely because of the Master's insistence: "He made his disciples get into the boat" (Mark 6:45) "and he said to them on that day, when evening had come, 'Let us cross over to the other side' " (Mark 4:35).

But what they feared, happened. "And there arose a great squall, and the waves were beating into the boat, so that the boat was now filling" (Mark 4:37). They were no doubt used to such weather and could put up with it. They steeled themselves to cope with the difficulties of the moment. But the Nazarene, a man from the hill country, still unaccustomed to this low atmospheric pressure at 760 feet below sea-level and tired out by a long day of preaching, had not been able to resist drowsiness; he was sleeping. Mark notes this detail: "he himself was in the stern of the boat, on the cushion, asleep" (4:38). This cushion can still be found today in the little fishing-boats: it is reserved for the guest, an amenity which our sailors will never use for themselves.

As he had been the cause of their difficulties, Jesus owed it to himself to rescue them from these difficulties. Wakened by their cries of alarm: " 'Master, does it not concern thee that we are perishing?' . . . he rebuked the wind, and said to the sea: 'Peace, be still.' And the wind fell and there came a great calm" (Mark 4:38-39).

Once again the good fishermen touch the supernatural at close range. Not yet having faith, "they feared exceedingly" (Mark 4:41).

This fear will become terror a few months later when they see Jesus walking on the waves: "they were utterly beside themselves," as Mark describes it (6:51). That time, too, Jesus had forced them to go out on the lake at night. But he had not gone with them; he had withdrawn "up the mountain by himself to pray" (Matthew 14:23). From up there, thanks to a beautiful moon in a cloudless sky, he could follow their slow progress, against the wind. This promontory, to which he had withdrawn, was a magnificent vantage point. Feeling himself a little responsible for the many difficulties he had occasioned, he comes down toward them, sympathetic and kind as ever: "and seeing them straining at the oars, for the wind was against them . . . he came to them . . . walking upon the sea" (Mark 6:48). His voice reassured them that he was not a ghost. "Then he got into the boat with them" (Mark 6:51) and "immediately the boat was at the land, towards which they were going" (John 6:21).

MULTIPLICATION OF THE LOAVES

The miracle we have just described took place after that of the "first multiplication of loaves." Let us not leave the shore of the lake without stopping a few moments to re-read the gospel text.

It will be still better if we read it at Tabgha, in the Church of the Multiplication of the Loaves, where the German Benedictine Fathers of the Dormition Abbey, in Jerusalem, have built a large monastery. One of the fathers will be glad to take you inside the church where there are some very fine mosaics, portraying the birds of the lake region. In the apse, near the altar, there is a somewhat cruder mosaic, depicting a basket containing five loaves, with a fish on either side of it. Apparently this is where the Christians of the fourth century venerated the memory of the first multiplication of the loaves (Mark 6:30-44).

The present site, located nearly two miles west of Capharnaum, answers well enough to Mark's description: "a desert place apart" (6:32), which is more easily accessible by land than by boat.[11]

In their haste, the good people had not taken along anything to eat. Today, as then, this would be one of those thin loaves of bread which we have already described, folded over two or three times. In the middle, the poor would put some olives or a bit of white cheese; the better-off, a fish or a piece of meat.

Among the thousands present that day, there were only a few who had been provident. And the disciples, after a search, ended by finding "five loaves and two fishes" (Mark 6:38). John says specifically that one such well-provided person was a "young boy" (John 6:9). Apparently his mother had given him five little loaves and two fishes that morning; and he, attracted by Jesus' gentle charm, had followed him this far from home.

Jesus thereupon orders the disciples to make the whole crowd "recline in groups on the green grass. And they reclined in groups of hundreds and fifties" (Mark 6:40). All these vivid little details tell us a great deal when we compare them with what we see today. The "green grass" shows the time of year: the beginning of summer, somewhere about the Passover, as John once again says specifically (6:4). The grass is always more abundant and thicker in this hot, well-watered region of the "Ghor." A little plot of land in this area will give a better yield than one many times its size in the cooler, drier regions.

The fact that the people reclined on the grass proves that

---

11. However, biblical scholars place the miracle rather on the east of the lake. Placing it on the west was from motives of convenience. It makes little difference.

Mount Tabor

Capharnaum

A Tomb with Circular Stone

Steps from the Cenacle to Cedron Valley

the rainy season was over since they certainly would not have stretched out on wet grass and in the mud.

They arranged themselves in groups of fifties or hundreds, no doubt by their home villages or neighborhoods. Even nowadays, when there are large public gatherings, it is essential to keep track of where each group comes from, if regrettable incidents are to be avoided.

The last point, mentioned only by Matthew (14:21), is a most natural thing in the East. "The number of those who had eaten was five thousand men, without counting women and children." No one would have ventured to count the women who had to eat by themselves and who almost certainly left before the end of the meal, taking the left-overs with them.

This same point is made again, exclusively by Matthew (15:38) when describing the second multiplication of the loaves: "Now those who had eaten were four thousand men, apart from children and women." For the Jewish evangelist, just as for the Oriental story-teller of today, women do not count nor are they counted.

MOUNT OF THE BEATITUDES

From Capharnaum, after our stop at Tabgha, it will be an easy matter to reach the Mount of the Beatitudes. From there, we shall look out over practically the whole lake. Here we can admire the "charter of the gospel," reproduced in chapters five, six and seven of Matthew. These "Beatitudes" and all the teaching that follows them are presented in the forceful expressions so familiar to our Eastern ears, so that popular memory would not fail to retain them. We must not forget that Jesus uttered them twenty centuries ago, and that there were no stenographers among his auditors.

These men preserved, more or less whole, the expressions that struck them most forcefully. With each adding a little touch of his own, the gospel writer has thus been able to reconstruct the teaching of the Master. It is in this way that, before Islam, the loveliest Arabic poetry (the "mouallakat") was learned by heart and handed down from generation to generation, until finally they were written down.

TABOR

If we take the route south towards Haifa and Jerusalem at the point where one re-enters the region of Tiberias along the route from Nazareth, we will be able to stop for some lingering moments at Tabor, "where it is good to be" (Mark 9:5).

From this mountain (almost seventeen hundred feet in height) we have one of the prettiest views in all Palestine. To the west we look over the fertile plain of Esdralon; and on the eastern side over the whole of the Jordan depression; and on both sides it is hemmed in with mountains. It is an enchanting landscape, quite different from the one we admired at the lake, and above all much more extensive, since we are on a promontory.

Let us reread the gospel account of the transfiguration which has been traditionally placed here since the fourth century. Doubtless it was after the oppressive heat of a summer's day, a little after midday that "Jesus took Peter, James and John and led them up a high mountain off by themselves" (Mark 9:2), exactly as our countrymen do today. Here we are in the solitude of the lovely basilica of Tabor or in the spacious hospice of the Franciscan fathers. We have left beneath us at the foot of the mountain the Moslem village of Dabourieh (population: about two thousand) where Jesus will shortly find his disciples arguing with the crowd gathered round the deaf-and-dumb possessed boy.

The little group of apostles, having reached the top of the mountain at sunset, would fill their lungs with deep breaths of the fresh air coming from the west, which we appreciate so much ourselves, especially after the stifling heat of the "Ghor" or of the coast. People today have no hesitation in sleeping out of doors in summer. As a matter of course they try to get away from their hot, stuffy houses. And we may reasonably suppose that the three disciples, tired from their climb, stretched out, wrapped in their cloaks, to try to refresh themselves with a little nap. They scarcely concerned themselves with Jesus, since they were used to seeing him spend a great part of his nights in prayer.

They were suddenly awakened (Luke 9:32) by a blinding light: Jesus "was transfigured before them. And his garments became shining, exceedingly white . . . And there appeared to them Elias with Moses, and they were talking, with Jesus" (Mark 9:3-4). It was not a dream: they were actually seeing this vision fully awake—this vision that they would never forget and that Peter and John will recall many years later.[12]

---

12. "For we were not following fictitious tales when we made known to you the power and coming of our Lord Jesus Christ, but we had been eyewitnesses of his grandeur . . . And this voice we ourselves

The first thought of Peter, the impetuous, was a conventional act of hospitality. He would be lacking in courtesy and consideration for Jesus and his guests, if he did not hasten to provide "three tents, one for thee, and one for Moses, and one for Elias" (cf. Mark 9:5). "For he did not know what to say, for they were struck with fear" (Mark 9:6).

Every time they are brought up against the supernatural at this stage of their training the poor apostles, still not endowed with that strong faith that Pentecost will bring them, are always seized with dread, bewilderment or terror, as we have had on several occasions to remark.

Let us, therefore, who have the grace of faith, receive devoutly this command: "This is my beloved Son, with whom I am well-pleased; hear him!" (Matthew 17:5). We can then come down from the holy mountain again, under the spell of the deep impression that Jesus has come near us and touched us with his grace, and we shall resume our road of life, lifted up and without fear (cf. Matthew 17:7).

---

heard borne from heaven when we were with him on the holy mount." (2 Peter, 1:16, 18).

". . . what we have heard, what we have seen with our eyes . . . the Eternal Life which was with the Father, and has appeared to us" (1 John 1:2).

CHAPTER TEN

VISITS AND FEASTS

Life in Palestine is divided, as elsewhere, between work, holidays, visits, and sleep. We have already had occasion to describe both men's and women's work. There remains then only for us to speak of visits and feasts: the gospel makes frequent reference to both, and always with the presumption that the customs involved are familiar to the reader.

WASHING OF THE FEET

Nowadays as formerly, in the villages or in tents, banquets and the main public gatherings take place in the evenings, for reasons already mentioned and explained.

The guests often come from a considerable distance. The first act of kindness offered them is the opportunity to wash their feet. There is, however, a tendency for this custom to disappear more and more, and I have had personal experience of it in only two villages. On our arrival, the lady of the house brought a basin full of lukewarm water and made preparations to wash our feet herself. Like Peter, I refused to let her do it, but I was very glad to wash my own feet in this refreshing water.

The point is that, even if the traveller is wearing shoes—and even more so if he is barefoot or simply wearing sandals and no socks—that fine, white, chalky dust of the village alleys sifts into his feet, and, especially on a hot day, causes severe discomfort. The obvious remedy for this is water. But it is not only to refresh himself that the traveller is given what he needs to wash his feet on arrival. Hygienic considerations are just as important, especially where running water is unknown. The importance of this first welcoming gesture of courteous hospitality will thus be readily appreciated.

The gospel has an extended account of this custom of washing the feet, and refers to it at other times. Let us think of the disciples of Jesus as guests for the paschal meal. It will then seem less unusual that Jesus would arise from the table, remove his cloak, and taking a linen cloth bind it about him. We are not astonished that he poured some water into a basin, washed the disciples' feet, and dried them with the towel that he had bound about him (John 13:4, 5).

In other texts, a simple reference is made to this obligatory rule of hospitality: "I came into your house; you gave me no water for my feet," said Jesus to his host, the Pharisee (Luke 7:44).

Elsewhere, Mary the sister of Lazarus, not content to wash the feet of Jesus with water, takes "a pound of ointment, genuine nard of great value, and anointed the feet of Jesus, and with her hair wiped his feet dry" (John 12:3).

BANQUETS

After the footwashing, guests read, chat, drink or eat. The men are kept apart from the women, who are usually busily engaged in preparing whatever is to be served to the men.

After receiving the kiss of welcome from his host, it is normal for the invited guest to greet those whom he meets with a kiss and an embrace. One is embraced by the beard ordinarily, for this is considered the noblest part of the face.

Our Lord complained about the fact that his host the Pharisee had neglected this rule of hospitality: "You gave me no kiss" (Luke 7:44).

Nowadays, in villages as yet untouched by modern customs, a low table is placed in the middle of the room and on it are set the various dishes. At each guest's place lies a large pancake-like bread, which will also serve as plate and spoon. A spoonful of rice, seasoned with sauce or sour milk is placed on a slice of this bread. The lamb is skilfully cut by hand and the host will sever a sizeable slice, which will be the main part of the meal. After a dozen mouthfuls the guest gets up to give his place to another, who will be served a new "pancake" bread, and so it goes on, until all the guests have been served. It is then the turn of the host and the members of his family, and there is now no objection to the women mixing with the men. During the banquet, the host will never sit down to table with his guests. He will serve them standing and see to it that they have everything they want.

Among the Bedouins and those who have similar customs—especially in Transjordan—a big platter is set in the midst of the guests. It contains a huge mound of rice or borgol (wheat-meal) topped off with sour milk or hot butter and on the top of the mound (called "mancaf") a whole sheep.

Each guest with a quick dextrous movement dips his fingers into the plate of rice and takes a fistful that he skilfully compresses into a large mouthful which he then eats. The same operation is repeated two or three times; then the guest helps himself to a generous portion of meat, after which he gives his place to another guest. In any case, it is rare for a guest to stay more than a few minutes at the table.

These meals are taken standing up or sitting on little square stools. When finished, the guest rejoins the other guests sitting in the nearby room or enjoying the fresh evening air outside. There the guests sit sipping their bitter coffee from special cups reserved for such occasions.

These details about local customs will help to make clearer the gospel texts in which frequent mention is made of meals and feasts.

The parable of the wedding feast (Matthew 22:1-14) takes for granted that the host is not at table with the guests (cf. v. 11: "Now the king went in to see the guests . . .").

The feast at the home of Levi (Luke 5:29-32) describes the motley crowd that always gathers at a feast: "a great gathering of publicans and of others, who were at the table with them," not to mention "the Pharisees and their scribes" who made no secret of their caustic criticisms.

It should be noted that these criticisms presuppose the still prevalent custom, already well-established in the Old Testament, of sealing friendships by a banquet (cf. Genesis 26:28-30: Abimelech and Isaac; Genesis 31:46-54: Laban and Jacob; Josue 9:14: Josue and the Gabaonites; 2 Samuel 3:20: David and Abner). "Do not forget that you have shared bread and salt" is a traditional Arab admonition to two friends who have fallen out. This brings to mind the expression a "covenant of salt" used in the Old Testament (Numbers 18:19; 2 Chronicles 13:5) to signify a very close alliance.

The Pharisees show their annoyance at having to eat with publicans and other sinners. They make it quite clear that they want, at all costs, to avoid being considered friends of people of this sort.

The "rich man who . . . feasted every day in splendid fashion" (Luke 16:19) is acting quite in character. Today, as then, feasts are the chief sign of wealth and importance. No one is really "wajih" (distinguished) unless he often entertains lavishly.

Is there any need to add that the erroneous addition in the Clementine Vulgate and certain Greek manuscripts, depicting the refusal of the rich man's attendants to give the poor Lazarus "what fell from the rich man's table," is in flat contradiction with Oriental customs? These left-overs are always given to the poor, especially if these latter are covered with "sores."

And, if there are no "beggars," the crumbs are eaten by the "dogs under the table" (Mark 7: 28) for there are always a large number in the village.

Only one custom seems to have changed in modern times: that of eating reclining. Nowhere are people to be seen eating "reclining" or stretched out on mats. Yet it seems that at the feasts to which the gospel alludes, the guests were resting on one arm (the left), the right remaining free to eat with. The guests would recline on three sides of the low table, set in the middle of the room, leaving the other side free to provide access for the waiters. The apparent discrepancy is cleared up, if it is remembered that the custom of eating "reclining" was not native to the Jews; it was a late borrowing from Greco-Roman practice.

One result of this custom was that a guest could only engage in conversation with his two or three nearest neighbors; the other guests could very well pay no attention to such conversations or simply could not hear them.

THE HEADMAN

It is strange to read in the gospel that Jesus was invited by Pharisees to dine with them on a number of occasions:

"One of the Pharisees invited him to dine with him" (Luke 7:36). "Now after he had spoken a Pharisee asked him to dine with him" (Luke 11:37); ". . . he had entered the house of one of the rulers of the Pharisees on the Sabbath to take food" (Luke 14:1).

In view of the hatred of the Pharisees for Jesus, the question arises as to why they invited him to eat at their homes. Our present-day customs provide a satisfactory answer. Indeed, they make quite clear that the Pharisees had to invite Jesus.

As a matter of fact, nowadays in the villages or among the Bedouins, the guests are invariably received at the home of the headman, the "moukhtar" (chosen one). Even if you have come to visit someone else, your host will take you to the "moukhtar," not out of stinginess or contempt, far from it—but out of respect for you, the guest. He fears he will otherwise not be fulfilling his duties of hospitality—while the "moukhtar" has everything needed to receive strangers properly.

The first thing the moukhtar does is to grind coffee with a pestle in the special carved ebony bowl. The charcoal fire is always lit at his place, with tall gleaming brass coffee urns nearby. When the fire goes out it is a signal that the reception is over. The clanging of the cups, while the coffee is being ground, is the rallying call for the people from the nearby tents or houses to come and greet the traveller-guest, to drink a cup of coffee with him and most probably join in the feast that will be offered him. It is a welcome occasion for the poor to enjoy a little change from their monotonous daily diet.

The traveller will stop at nightfall in whatever village he has reached and the moukhtar, regardless of his personal attitude toward the visitor, will invite him to dine and spend the night at his house. This seems to be what we should understand by a gospel text like: ". . . . he entered the house of one of the rulers of the Pharisees" (Luke 14:1). This leading man was no other than the moukhtar of today and Jesus could not choose but go to his house; nor could the leading man refuse to receive Jesus, no matter how much he might dislike him.

But, though forced to receive Jesus, the Pharisee would find ways to show his contempt, by being rude to his guest and offending against the rules of hospitality—which no present-day "moukhtar," to our knowledge, would ever do; and Jesus does not hesitate to reproach him for this publicly.

Let us pause a moment in order to grasp the meaning of that wonderful scene reported in Luke 7:36–50:

"Now one of the Pharisees asked him to dine with him." As this was a time when Jesus "was journeying through towns and villages, preaching and proclaiming the good

news of the kingdom of God" (Luke 8:1) from Nain to
Capharnaum, it was only natural that he would have to
stop often for the night. On one of these occasions he was
obliged to seek shelter at the home of this Pharisee
"moukhtar," who in turn was obliged to invite him to a
meal.

"And behold, a woman in the town who was a sinner"
came in, perhaps Mary Magdalene (cf. Luke 8:2); this
would place the feast at Magdala, the present-day Migdal,
a few miles east of Capharnaum. "Upon learning that he
was at table in the Pharisee's house": the arrival of Jesus
and his disciples could not pass unnoticed. Plenty of gossip
would be circulating, and many too would have words of
praise for this rabbi. All this the woman would have heard
at the well, where she had come before nightfall to chat
with the other women of the village, while she drew water.
She would have no trouble finding out where Jesus was, for
he could only be at the home of the moukhtar, a Pharisee.

She "brought an alabaster jar of ointment": nothing more
natural for a converted sinner than to purify, as it were,
what had been for her an occasion of sin or a bait for
accomplices in sin.

"Standing behind him at his feet, she began to bathe his
feet with her tears, and wiped them with the hair of her
head, and kissed his feet, and anointed them with ointment."

Thus, this woman slips into the banquet hall without
attracting too much attention. The very fact that she comes
in indicates that she was no longer in the first flush of
youth for a young woman would never have had the
courage to enter a banquet hall, as we have already noted

when speaking of how the mother of Jesus came in at the wedding feast at Cana.

The door of the room was always open to facilitate the constant coming and going of the cousins and relatives of the host, who were busy serving food and drink to the guests. This woman had easily slipped in among them without arousing any suspicion. She edges along the walls, looks the guests over carefully and finally recognizes Jesus reclining next to Simon. There is no chance of speaking to him. She could not go out into the middle of the room where she would have hindered those serving and where her presence would not have been tolerated. So she stays close to the wall, scarcely noticed by Jesus and those of his companions who were near him; "and standing behind him at his feet,"—the gospel text is precise in its description.

Her tears of repentance do not prevent her from noticing right away the fine white dust which still covers Jesus' feet. If she had been at her own home such a breach of courtesy would not have been tolerated. She would have repaired the oversight, whether deliberate or involuntary, of the master of the feast, by bringing lukewarm water and a towel. But here she could not risk losing the few minutes she had to be so close to Jesus. Her freely-flowing tears must take the place of water, her hair serve as a towel, and, as a sign of respectful affection, she covers Jesus' feet with kisses and anoints them with the perfume.

The whole thing must have happened with the anxious haste of a person who is afraid of being noticed too quickly. She certainly knew that guests usually stayed only a few minutes at table.

But Jesus knows how to prolong the joy that she feels

at being at his feet and he begins a conversation which will keep anyone from rising to leave.

He reads the inner thoughts of his host, who is saying to himself, "This man, were he a prophet, would surely know just who and what manner of woman this is who is touching him, for she is a sinner." Divining his thoughts, Jesus says to him: "Simon, I have something to say to you." It is easy to visualize Jesus leaning over quite far to Simon, tapping him gently on the shoulder, and asking for his undivided attention.

Turning around somewhat—a movement we shall see a little later in the beloved John—he replies, "Master, speak."

Jesus addresses him in the oriental style that delights in circumlocutions which lead to a reproach never administered directly. He tells Simon a little allegory that, at first hearing, arouses no suspicion of the speaker: "A certain money-lender had two debtors; the one owed five hundred denarii, the other fifty. As they had no means of paying, he forgave them both. Which of them, therefore, will love him more?"

The Pharisee did not see clearly. He did not understand the comparison of himself, the "pure" according to the Law, who hardly owed fifty, with the great sinner that Jesus was pointing to, with one who, overloaded with sins, surely owed five hundred denarii. The Master has come to bring forgiveness. There is no doubt that the great sinner will be pardoned with love. He who was afraid that he would be dismissed or reprimanded will even be acknowledged, so that he will not fear to show himself in public. But this will be less likely for the proud man who believes that he has only good deeds to offer God. (See the parable of the Pharisee and the Publican.)

Naively unsuspecting, "Simon answered and said: 'He, I suppose, to whom he forgave more.'" The question as put by Jesus could not be answered any other way.

Hence, Jesus' approving reply: "Thou hast judged rightly."

Then he begins this severe reprimand:

"And turning to the woman, he said to Simon: 'Dost thou see this woman?'"—this woman, whom in your heart you despise holds in my esteem a higher place than you! And Jesus swiftly paints for his host the picture of all the rudenesses Simon has committed and which the woman whom he despises has repaired a hundredfold.

First act of rudeness: "I came into thy house; thou gavest me no water for my feet; but she has bathed my feet with tears and has wiped them with her hair."

Second act of rudeness which she has so admirably atoned for: "Thou gavest me no kiss; but she has not ceased to kiss my feet."

Third act of rudeness on your part: "Thou didst not anoint my head with oil; but she has anointed my feet with ointment."

Jesus could have added the fourth act of rudeness of the haughty host: "Thou ought not to have sat down at table with me but rather to have considered it an honor to serve me!" but he spares him this fourth reproach, as too personal.

The conclusion was inescapable, humiliating for the Pharisee and entirely to the advantage of the "sinner": "Wherefore I say to thee, her sins, many as they are, shall be forgiven her because she has loved much." By now the Pharisee no longer has any trouble completing the comparison: if the scandalous woman is pardoned, he is not. Or scarcely so! "He to whom little is forgiven, loves little."

The woman had doubtless grasped only snatches of the conversation; she was waiting for a word of comfort which she hoped to hear before she went away, and is richly rewarded: "And he said to her: 'Thy sins are forgiven.'"

The guests began to get up from table, following the lead of Jesus, who had stood up to speak to the woman. They hear the last word of pardon. Not having followed the whole conversation which had just taken place between the Pharisee and Jesus, they are astonished at such audacity and "began to say within themselves: 'Who is this man, who even forgives sins!'" Jesus takes no notice. He leaves it to his host to explain to the guests all that Jesus had said to him privately. But Jesus wants to reassure the startled woman; so he dismisses her with a look she will never forget and which will keep her forever bound to her beloved Rabbi: "But he said to the woman: 'Thy faith has saved thee; go in peace.'"

THE PASCHAL MEAL

Unquestionably the most important of the numerous banquets mentioned in the gospels is the "Eucharistic Banquet," of which all four evangelists write, each adding details omitted by the others. The relevant passages are: Matthew 26:17-29; Mark 14:12 ff.; Luke 22:7-23; John 13:1 ff. The various customs we have described will help us better to understand these texts.

The entire thirteenth chapter of John is devoted to a description of the washing of the feet and Peter's vividly reported answers. Mark (14:18) specifies that the apostles were reclining at table; and he is likewise the one who describes the room where the feast took place: the owner "will show you a large upper room furnished; there make ready for us." This detail indicates that the owner was a man of some wealth, since he has an upper room "furnished," that is to say, provided with the mats and cushions for the guests.

The detail furnished by John, "he whom Jesus loved, was reclining at Jesus' bosom," accurately indicates the place at table of the beloved disciple. Since John would be reclining with his back to Jesus, he would have to turn to speak to him. Peter must have been reclining further away, since, in order to speak to John, he "beckoned to him" (John 13:24) to catch his attention.

We imagine here, too, as in the scene of the Pharisee and the scandalous woman, that none of the others can hear the intimate conversation between Jesus and John, and, until the moment the betrayer leaves, "none of those at the table understood why he said this to him" (John 13:28).

Finally, Matthew (26:20) gives the exact time of day at which the paschal meal began: "when evening arrived, he reclined at table with the twelve disciples": and John notes (13:29) that at the time when Judas went out: "It was night." The explanation is that the banquet, which, as always, had begun in the evening at sunset, had already lasted some considerable time. There had been the washing of the feet and the first preparations which preceded the institution of the Eucharist. The meal is undoubtedly

8

finished and the disciples are beginning to get up from table, when Jesus says his touching farewell: "Little children, yet a little while I am with you" (John 13:33 ff.). There follows a lively conversation in which Peter, Thomas and Philip take part.

Then, "after reciting a hymn" of the Hallel (Matthew 26:30), Jesus says to the disciples: "Arise; let us go from here" (John 14:31).

The disciples now follow the Master down the slope of Mount Sion, where the upper room was located, to make their way, after crossing the Cedron, as was their custom, to the Mount of Olives (cf. Luke 22:39). At the foot of the Mount of Olives, "they . . . came to a country place called Gethsemane" (Mark 14:32). It is here that Jesus tells his disciples to stop and "Pray, that you may not enter into temptation" (Luke 22:40). On the way to Gethsemane, Jesus saw the vines in the light of the full moon. He was familiar enough with vinedressing to know that the branches pruned from the main vine at the end of the winter, and which the little band was doubtless treading underfoot, would bear no more fruit. And quite spontaneously following out this thought, he tells his disciples who are pressing anxiously about him this wonderful parable: "I am the true vine, and my Father is the vinedresser. . . . As the branch cannot bear fruit of itself unless it remain on the vine, so neither can you unless you abide in me" (John 15:1, 4).

CHAPTER ELEVEN

DEATH AND BURIAL

Death is the inescapable end of the road of life, to which all of us must sooner or later come. It entails a series of ceremonies and customs which vary from country to country, from age to age. We should know them in order to explain the frequent references of the gospel writers to death and burial.

PRESENT-DAY CUSTOMS

The first thing to be noted is that in tropical countries the deceased is kept only a few hours: one who has died in the morning will be buried in the afternoon; one who has died during the night will be buried toward the following noon. During the hottest season I have often noticed during the services that the body was decomposing, even after this very brief lapse of time.

Customs surrounding funerals are entirely different in the more or less modernized towns and cities from those in the villages. It is in these latter, with their more conservative practices, that we must look for the customs which are most akin to those of gospel times.

In the villages Christians and non-Christians observe quite different customs. Among Christians the deceased, dressed in his best clothes, is laid out on a bed if there is one, or, if not, on a mat in the middle of the one-room house, or in the main room, if the family has several.

The women relatives are grouped around the remains; the nearest relatives always stay quite close to the deceased. Their hair is disheveled, their face sometimes covered with dust. In certain more primitive localities, I have seen the women tear their clothes and partly expose their breasts; but this is rather rare.

In the midst of these women crowded together, some seated, some standing, there is a professional woman "mourner." She keeps repeating in a monotonous rhythm certain phrases, which all the women take up, breaking into tears and loud sobs each time a newcomer enters to join the group.

Meanwhile, the men are sitting in a nearby room talking sometimes of the deceased and often of other things, sipping the bitter coffee served them on their arrival.

All fast until the actual funeral. For this, the clergy come into the room where the deceased is laid out, recite there the liturgical prayers, while the women withdraw to make room for the men who will act as pallbearers. Then the funeral procession sets out, with the clergy at its head, followed by the deceased borne by the pallbearers. The men walk behind these while the women bring up the rear still singing their sad, monotonous songs.

At the church where the funeral services are to be sung I have sometimes seen the close relatives sit down near the coffin in the middle of the nave, and continue their lamentations in a disarray which I have had to reprimand publicly.

Usually the men occupy the front part of the nave, while the women stay further behind. In other places, especially in the towns where the custom of having "mourners" has been discontinued, the women do not accompany the deceased to the church at all.

The funeral service over, the deceased is again taken up by the pallbearers and carried to the cemetery, with only the men going along. Generally all the men of the village accompany the deceased, particularly if he is a poor man. On their return the meal which neighbor families have prepared is served; the men, who have been fasting till now, eat by themselves; the women eat afterwards.

The cemetery is always located outside the village, quite far from the settled area. The deceased is simply buried in the group, especially in the poor villages. The custom of family vaults, though introduced in some large towns and cities, is unknown in the villages of today. For several days after the funeral the bereaved receive condolences. The women will not leave the house except to go to the requiem masses which are sung on the third, ninth and fortieth day and again six months and a year after. In many places they will not even go to Sunday mass and will refrain from all visiting during the six months immediately following a death. The custom of wearing mourning has been introduced pretty well everywhere; and black will be taken off only when the closest surviving relative of the deceased authorizes it.

Let us try, with the aid of the customs we have just described, to visualize the various scenes in the gospel relating to the dead and to burial.

GOSPEL SCENES

The gospel gives several accounts of deaths and of resurrections:

In Luke (7:1-17) there is the story of the resurrection of the son of the widow of Naïn: Naïn is undoubtedly the present-day village of Nène or Naina southeast of Nazareth and about twenty miles from Capharnaum. Today this village is entirely Moslem, but in it, on the road from Tiberias to Jerusalem, there is a little Christian church, easily recognizable by its red tiles. The modern pronunciation of Naine has in it no echo of Naïm and we should keep to the spelling which is more and more widespread today and speak of the "widow of Naïn" rather than the "widow of Naïm."

The proper translation of verse 11 is: "*Soon afterward*, he went to a town called Naïn." Those translators who, instead of "soon afterward" use "the next day," do not realize that a caravan like that of our Lord could not cover the twenty-odd miles between Capharnaum and Naïn in a single day.

"And as he drew near the gate of the town": then as now the deceased was carried quite a distance outside the village, always beyond the entire settled area.

"A large gathering from the town was with her": the whole village accompanies the deceased. The latter is carried by the young men, with the older men going ahead and the weeping women following after, among them the widow, the mother of the deceased. Jesus is touched by the sight of her and asks the widow "not to weep." For Lazarus, he will weep himself, together with Martha and Mary!

Jesus leaves the mourners after this word of encouragement to the widow. He goes a little ahead, rejoins the men, lays his hand on the coffin and the procession stops. The crowd surrounds him, curious to see what will happen. Indeed, two crowds mingle, that accompanying Jesus and the "large gathering from the town," who were walking in the funeral procession.

"And he said: 'Young man, I say to thee, arise!' And he who was dead sat up . . ." As always, on contact with the supernatural, "fear seized upon all" and all became apostles, proclaiming the power of this "great prophet" who "has risen among us."

Another resurrection, that of Jairus' daughter, took place before the funeral, in fact only a few hours after her death. As nowadays, the dead girl's house was full of people, "weeping and mourning for her" (Luke 8:52), or as Mark describes them, "a people weeping and wailing greatly" (5:38). The dead girl is in a special room, which indicates that Jairus, "a ruler of the synagogue" (Luke 8:41) owned quite a spacious house. Mark notes most precisely, on the basis of the exact information of Peter, who was taken along into this special room, that Jesus "entered in where the girl was lying" (Mark 5:40). The clearing of the room, reported by Mark (5:40), becomes readily understandable when we consider that the room in question is the one in which the young girl, stretched out on a pallet, is surrounded by mourners. It could never be an easy thing to send them away; necessarily, it took a certain amount of time.

Luke (8:51) says that Jesus "came to the house" and let no one enter with him "except Peter, James and John, and the girl's father and mother." This passage too must be understood in terms of the customs that have just been described. People often remained out side because the room was too small and too stifling. But most would have followed Jesus if he had not prevented it.

In the miracle referred to before, Jesus "touched the coffin." In this instance, he "here took the dead girl's hand." Direct contact is the source of the infusion of life. We must prepare our souls for the grace of the sacraments, and above all for the grace of the Eucharist, a sensible sign, the bearer of Divinity.

"Her spirit returned" (Luke 8:55), and the "young girl rose up immediately and began to walk" (Mark 5:42). Once more the reaction is still one of amazement: "And they were utterly amazed" (Mark 5:42).

The resurrection that would have had the greatest reverberation is that of Lazarus. This is undoubtedly because of its proximity to Jerusalem, and the importance of the death of one who returns to life. The whole story is told at length in John (11:1-46). The Byzantine liturgy has consecrated to him the vigil of Palm Sunday, which is called "Lazarus Saturday" in the liturgical books.

Here, too, it is easy to reconstruct the course of events:
Bethany is about four miles east of Jerusalem. Today it is the entirely Moslem village of Beit-Anya, dominated by the orphanage of the Daughters of Charity. The Franciscan fathers have just built a splendid church there on the supposed site of Lazarus' tomb.

Jesus had often been the guest of Lazarus and his two sisters. When their brother fell gravely ill, the sisters hastened to send a messenger to Jesus, to tell him that "he whom thou lovest is sick" (John 11:3). The two sisters did not doubt for a moment that Jesus, who had cured so many sick people before their eyes, would lose no time in curing their brother too.

Besides, they know that, with their brother dead, Jesus would not be able to have easy access to their home, located so conveniently near to Jerusalem. He could not come to the home of two women living alone. And they knew he was fond of them and their brother. The gospel notes at this point: "Now Jesus loved Martha and her sister Mary and Lazarus."

Jesus' reply to the delicately worded but pressing request of the two sisters was undoubtedly calculated to reassure them: "This sickness is not unto death," but there was no mention of what they hoped for: the news that he would come at once. On the contrary, Jesus "remained two more days in the same place" (John 11:6), across the Jordan (John 10:40).

When he wants to take his disciples back into Judea, where "just now the Jews were seeking to stone him" (11:8), it is not without anxiety that he decides to have them follow him. This decision taken, "they do not stumble" (11:9), for they are following the light.

On the contrary, if they had withdrawn from him, the true "light of this world," they would then have stumbled, as we stumble so often over the pebbles and the innumerable stones along our little paths "when we walk in the night."

Jesus and his disciples crossed the depression of the "Ghor," which is more than eleven hundred feet below sea level. They then climbed the mountains of Juda to the point where, at a height of more than twenty-one hundred feet, Bethany is located. This route was taken very often by the Master in his younger days, for it was by this route that the holy family journeyed on its way from Nazareth to Jerusalem.

Perhaps he stayed here overnight on the way to Jericho, which lay a seven or eight hour walk from Jerusalem. And when he arrived at Bethany, he "found Lazarus already four days in the tomb" (11:17). His group, as it comes from the east, meets "many of the Jews" coming from the west, from Jerusalem and its environs, "to comfort Martha and Mary on account of their brother" (11:19).

At the entrance to the village Jesus pauses, and Martha would immediately be made aware of his arrival. She is eager to "go to meet him" (11:20). Contrary to all normal customs, which would prohibit any kind of public conference, this woman speaks and listens to things of the greatest importance (see John 11:21-27).

Jesus was still "at the place where Martha had met him" (John 11:31), at the edge of the village, probably on the road to the cemetery. That is why, when the people saw Mary going in that direction, they "followed her, saying: 'She is going to the tomb to weep there' " (John 11:30-31).

Jesus was moved almost to tears at the sight of Mary and the Jews weeping. He asks to see the tomb. All go with him and when they reach it, the cave is opened by rolling away the stone which lay against it.

" 'Because of the people who stand round . . . that they may believe that thou hast sent me' (John 11:42). When he had said this, he cried out with a loud voice: 'Lazarus, come forth!' " The miracle is worked; the dead man is raised to life. The hatred of the Pharisees is only intensified: "So from that day forth their plan was to put him to death" (John 11:53) and to do away with Lazarus along with Jesus.

JESUS' TOMB

The Pharisees almost immediately found a chance to seize Jesus and to have Pilate condemn him to death. It was Friday, the eve of the Passover. Jesus died about three o'clock in the afternoon and was taken down from the cross about five, an hour before sunset and the beginning of the Sabbath rest: "and the Sabbath was drawing on" as Luke (23:54) puts it.

The burial takes place quickly. The body of Jesus is laid in a vault which Joseph of Aramathea had had cut out of the rock nearby (Matthew 27:60). This vault was no doubt similar to those rich men's vaults that can still be seen at Jerusalem, of which the most famous is the so-called "tomb of the Kings." It resembles a little house of several rooms, cut into the face of the rock. One of the rooms serves as an entrance hall and the others contain the recesses in which the bodies of the deceased were laid. The tomb had only one entrance, usually fairly low, before which was rolled a huge stone, similar to a large mill-stone, which closed it off.

The body of Jesus "wrapped . . . in a clean linen cloth" (Matthew 27:59), "wrapped . . . in linen cloths with the spices" (John 19:40), was laid in the inner room. Joseph of Aramathea, no doubt with Nicodemus helping him, "rolled a large stone to the entrance of the tomb, and departed" (Matthew 27:60) out of respect for the Sabbath. The holy women who had followed Jesus "were looking on and saw where he was laid" (Mark 15:47) and how his body had been interred (cf. Luke 23:56).

Calvary and the tomb were both outside the city.

RESURRECTION

Jesus' death was only the preparation for his resurrection, just as our death will be in fact only a passing into true life.

It will form a fitting conclusion to this study of life in Jesus' native land, if we study for a moment the scenes connected with the Resurrection which the gospel writers describe, each adding his own details.

Friday evening, while Jesus' body was being laid away in the tomb, his soul was on its way to limbo, to announce to the souls of the just, waiting there, the approach of the hour of their entry into heaven.

At dawn on Sunday, the holy women carried bands and spices to complete the embalming of the body of the Lord, which had been hastily attended to Friday evening, for want of time. Meanwhile Jesus had already risen and, doubtless, had gone to console his mother by showing himself first to her. The gospel does not report this meeting but the whole liturgical tradition supposes it:

"Regina coeli, laetare!" sings the Latin Church.

"An angel of the Lord" came down from heaven, and drawing near "rolled back the stone and sat upon it." The earthquake and the sight of the angel terrified the guards who "became like dead men" (Matthew 28:4) and then fled.

The women, on their arrival, are astonished to see the stone rolled away and the tomb open. Mary of Magdalene runs to tell Simon Peter and John (John 20:1-10). These latter verify the disappearance of the body and see the cloths and the shroud. On her return, Mary sees, on looking into the tomb, two angels. Then she recognizes Jesus himself, who calls her by her name: "Mary!" "Master!" she replies, and in obedience to the command Jesus gives her, she goes to tell the disciples that she has seen the Lord (John 20:11-18).

The other holy women, to whom the angels had announced Jesus' resurrection, were going back "in fear and great joy" and ran to tell his disciples. And behold, Jesus met them, saying, 'Hail'" (Matthew 28:8-9).

Jesus appeared next to the two disciples from Emmaus, who were leaving Jerusalem. They had heard the "tales" of the women and the results of the visit of Peter and John to the tomb. But they still did not believe; rather they seem disappointed and discouraged (Luke 24:13-34). "We were hoping" (Luke 24:21), they told Jesus. While they were retracing their steps to Jerusalem with the desire of sharing their new-found joy and faith with the others, Jesus had appeared to Peter alone (Luke 24:34).

Toward the end of this Sunday evening, "though the doors where the disciples gathered had been closed for fear of the Jews" (John 20:19), Jesus appears to all the assembled disciples, with the exception of Thomas, who was absent. He reassures them, reproaches them for their lack of faith, eats with them (Luke 24:36-43), and confers the Holy Spirit on them.

A week later he appears again to all the disciples together

and this time Thomas is present. Jesus reproaches Thomas for his obstinacy in not believing and calls blessed those who believe without having seen (John 20:24-29).

Later, he appeared in Galilee (Matthew 28:16) and on the shores of the Lake of Tiberias (John 21:1-23). There, in the wonderful surroundings of Galilee, which he knew and loved so well, he confirmed Peter in his primacy and foretold to him that he would be a martyr.